CHILD IN THE CITY:
PLANNING COMMUNITIES FOR CHILDREN AND THEIR FAMILIES

Child
in the city

Planning Communities for Children & their Families

Kristin N. Agnello, RPP, MCIP

This work is licensed under the Creative Commons Attribution-NonCommercial-ShareAlike 4.0 International License. To view a copy of this license, visit http://creativecommons.org/licenses/by-nc-sa/4.0/ or send a letter to Creative Commons, PO Box 1866, Mountain View, CA 94042, USA.

Published by Plassurban, Victoria, British Columbia, Canada
June 2020
www.plassurban.com

Disclaimer: Plassurban has made every reasonable effort to ensure the accuracy of this toolkit, but does not guarantee, and assumes no liability for, the accuracy or completeness of the information or its suitability for any particular purpose. It is the responsibility of users to apply their professional knowledge in the use of the information contained in this document, in the context of applicable local policies and regulations. Photos of planning and architectural elements are shown as examples only and the illustration or description of any products, services, or organizations in this toolkit does not imply endorsement by the author, contributors, or BC Housing.

Cover photograph ©istockphoto.com/oska25

ISBN: 978-1-989985-01-4

ACKNOWLEDGEMENTS

We gratefully acknowledge the financial support of BC Housing through the Building Excellence Research & Education Grants Program.

Plassurban is grateful for the participation of numerous residents, housing providers, and businesses from across the Capital Regional District. We received input from a wide range of citizens, professionals, and stakeholders, including planners, urban designers, housing providers, developers, architects, educators, mortgage brokers, realtors, and developers. Special thanks to Bill Brown for his thorough review and thoughtful commentary on the initial draft of this book. We are grateful to those who devoted their time to sharing their experiences, insights, feedback, and comments regarding the context of our local communities, including:

Wilma Leung	BC Housing
Karen Williams	BC Housing
Steven Chan	BC Housing
Leigh Greenius	BC Housing
Michael Kierszenblat	BC Housing
Sheryl Peters	BC Housing
Maya Korbynn	BC Housing
Alison James	City of Victoria
Lindsay Milburn	City of Victoria
Alison Verhagen	Town of Sidney
Corey Newcomb	Town of Sidney
Bill Brown	Township of Esquimalt
Alex Tang	Township of Esquimalt
Fred Billingham	Township of Esquimalt
Janany Nagulan	Township of Esquimalt
Pearl Barnard	Township of Esquimalt
Trevor Parkes	Township of Esquimalt
Tricia DeMacedo	Township of Esquimalt
Yolanda Meijer	Habitat for Humanity
Dr. Tamara Plush	UNICEF Consultant
Diana Studer	HDR Architecture Associates, Inc.
Steve Woolrich	Rethink Urban (CPTED Consultant)
Luke Mari	Aryze Developments (Proforma Review)
Chelsey Jersak	Situate, Inc. (Technical Peer Review)

CONTENTS

Acknowledgements iii
Preamble v

PART I: INTRODUCTION   1

1. **WHY PLAN FOR CHILDREN?**   3
2. **BASIC NEEDS OF CHILDREN**   3

PART II: POLITICS, POLICY AND THE FUTURE   9

3. **PLANNERS' TOOLKIT**   11

4. **POLICY MEASURES**   14
   Official Community Plans and Neighbourhood Plans 14
   Missing Middle Policy 17
   Secondary Suites Policies and Programs 19
   Housing First Policies for Surplus Public Land 21
   Child and Youth Consultation Policy 23
   Full Spectrum CPTED Policy 25

5. **REGULATORY MEASURES**   27
   Missing Middle Zoning 28
   Inclusionary Zoning 30
   Performance Zoning 32
   Density Bonusing 34
   Residential Rental Tenure Bylaw 36

6. **FINANCIAL MEASURES**   38
   Development Levies and Fee Waivers 38
   Property Tax Exemptions 40
   Municipal Land Banks 42
   Partnering Policy with Investment 43

7. **PARTNERSHIPS AND ALTERNATIVE DELIVERY METHODS**   45
   Fast Tracking the Development Approval Process 45
   Housing Agreements 47
   Municipal Children's Advocate 49
   Support Capacity within the Non-profit Housing Sector 51

8 THE TRANSACTIONAL NATURE OF PLANNING POLICY 53
Proformas 54

PART III: DESIGN GUIDELINES - BUILDING, BLOCK, CITY 61

9 DEVELOPMENTAL STAGES 63
Early Childhood (0-4 years) 64
School-Age Children (5-12) 65
Adolescents (10-19) 66
Young Adults (15-24) 68

10 DESIGN GUIDELINES 69
Principle 1 – Housing Diversity 73
Principle 2 – Built Form and Unit Design 76
Principle 3 – Sustainability 83
Principle 4 – Private Amenities 85
Principle 5 – Local Character and Context 88
Principle 6 – Landscape 90
Principle 7 – Full Spectrum CPTED 92
Principle 8 – Public Amenities 94
Principle 9 – Transportation Networks 99

PART IV: PARTICIPATORY PLANNING WITH CHILDREN 105

11 AGE-APPROPRIATE CONSULTATION 108
Engagement with Young Children, Parents, and Caregivers (0-4 years old) 108
Engaging with School-Age Children (5-12 years old) 112
Engaging with Adolescents (10-19 years old) 116
Children: Our Present, Our Future 119

Appendix A: Community Assessment Checklist 123
Appendix B: Building Assessment Checklist 135
Appendix C: Hypothetical Proformas 141

Glossary 149
Bibliography

PREAMBLE

"Give us – your children – a good today.
We will, in turn, give you a good tomorrow."
Toukir Ahmed, 16, Bangladesh[1]

For my young daughters, our community is part of their identity. It teaches them, challenges them, inspires them, and shapes their memories. A well-designed community allows children to learn as they go: exploring the nooks and crannies of the local parks, visiting with neighbours, watching wild bunnies and birds, and discovering each day's treasures along the shoreline. They like the places that support their independence – where they can choose to join in with others, search for wild berries, or simply sit alone with their thoughts and watch the action. My daughters dislike the fancy, newly-built oceanfront playground, preferring the smaller, community park that is sheltered from the wind and which they access via a "secret" treed catwalk, skirting the edges of neighbours' properties - hidden enough that they can explore independently, but within sight and reach of the safety of home. Watching my children has shaped my own understanding of the built environment and has shown me, time and again, how community design, policies, and amenities have the potential to shape relationships and either support children's growth and independence, or perpetuate dependence, frustration, and isolation.

Child and family-friendly communities acknowledge that an environment that addresses the needs of children – who have limited independent mobility, experience, and autonomy – is one that is friendlier and more accessible to people of all ages and abilities. This toolkit has been developed collaboratively, with voluntary input from local governments, non-profit housing organizations, architects, urban designers, urban planners, developers, real estate specialists, researchers, and educators.

This toolkit is not intended to exclude adults and seniors, but rather to provide a lens through which planners, designers, and policy-makers can support child and family-friendly development practices that have positive intergenerational benefits. To plan our cities in a way that enables children to be co-authors of their own communities is key to a sustainable – and inclusive – future. If the city tells a story of experience, opportunity, and ownership, then its design should enable all citizens to write their own story.

PART I: INTRODUCTION

"Let children be the co-authors of their communities."
Mara Mintzer[2]

The world is currently facing the largest wave of urbanization in history. With over half of the global population currently living in cities – a number that is projected to rise to nearly seventy percent by 2050[3] – it is critical that cities be co-designed to be inclusive and accessible, thereby meeting the needs of all residents, including the most vulnerable. As the global population continues to grow, conservative estimates predict that, by 2030, six out of ten urban residents will be under the age of eighteen[4]. In the 2016 census, Statistics Canada counted nearly one million children aged 19 or under living in communities across British Columbia – just over 20% of the total population. Of these children, nearly 15% were aged 14 and under[5]. For urban planners, architects, developers, and policy-makers, the question is not whether children will continue to live in urban communities, but how. We are entering a critical era - a tipping point of concentrated urban development, population growth, economic strain, and devastating environmental degradation.

INTRODUCTION

FAMILY demographics

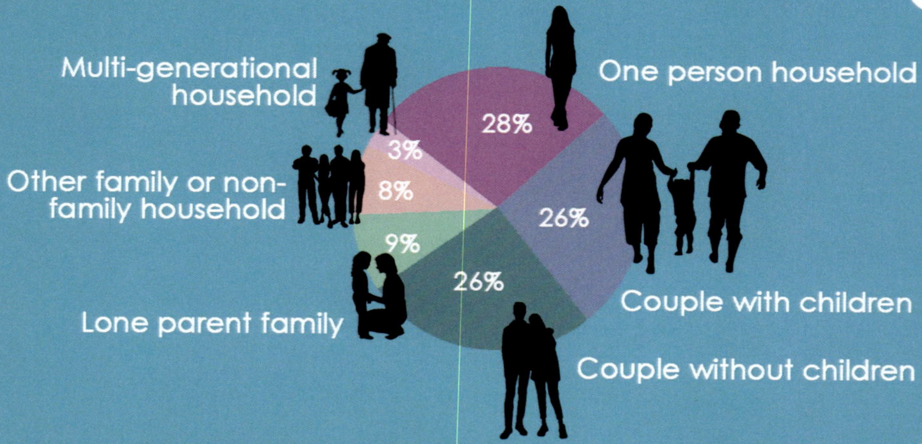

HOUSEHOLD COMPOSITIONS

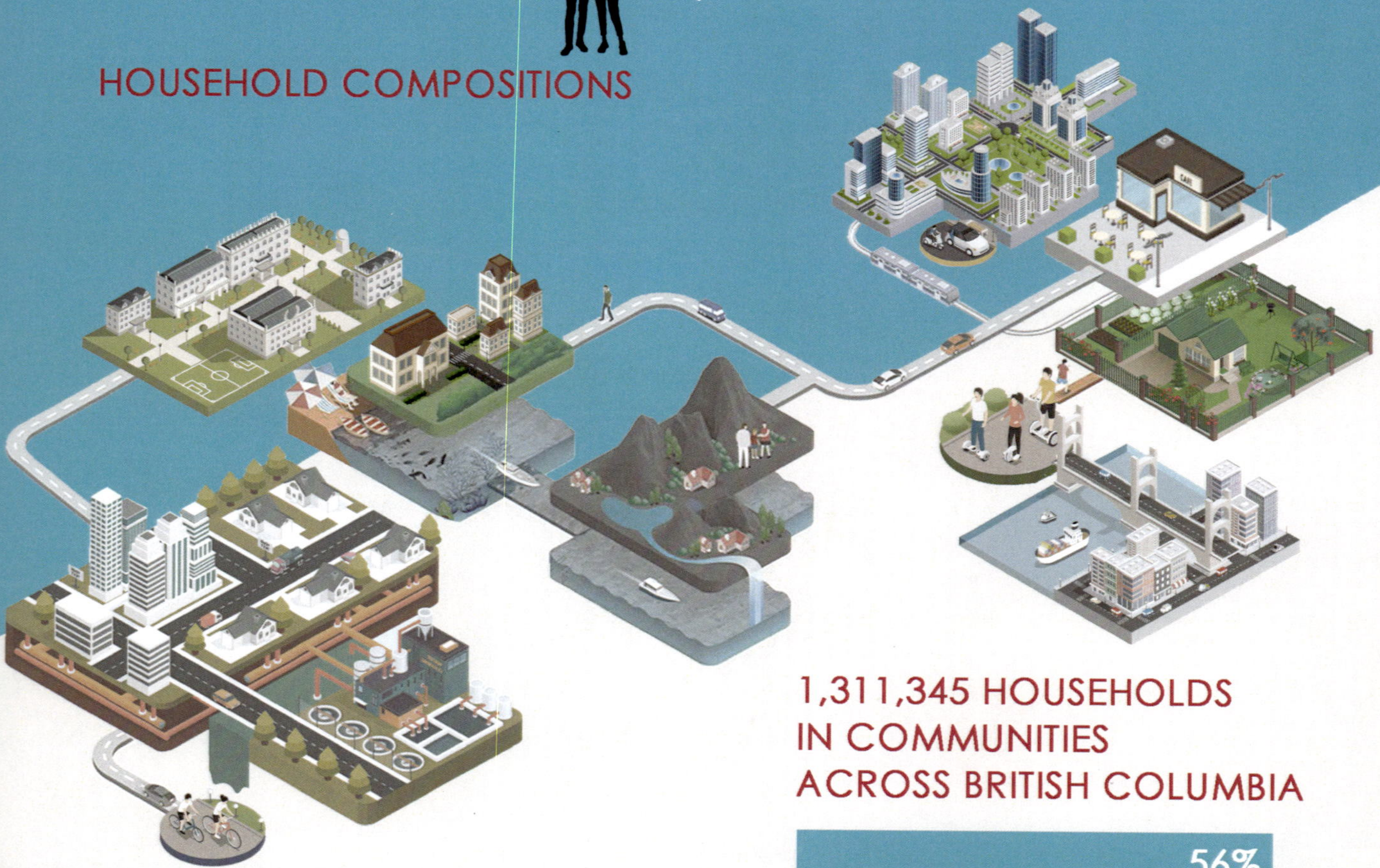

- Multi-generational household — 3%
- Other family or non-family household — 8%
- Lone parent family — 9%
- Couple without children — 26%
- Couple with children — 26%
- One person household — 28%

1,311,345 HOUSEHOLDS IN COMMUNITIES ACROSS BRITISH COLUMBIA

56% have children living in the home

27% of family households are led by lone parents

79% of lone parent families are headed by women

1   WHY PLAN FOR CHILDREN?

Children are disproportionately vulnerable to the dangers of urban life, including pollution, poverty, crime, or traffic. Like "canaries in a coal mine," children reveal the inequities and imbalance of the built environment precisely because of their vulnerability. As Enrique Peñalosa writes:

One common measure of how clean a mountain stream is is to look for trout. If you find the trout, the habitat is healthy. It's the same way with children in a city. Children are a kind of indicator species. If we can build a successful city for children, we will have a successful city for all people[6].

The visible presence of children – both with and independent from their parents – can give planners, designers, and policy-makers valuable clues about the safety, accessibility, and social cohesion of a community. A well-designed community provides opportunities for children to explore their world, make mistakes, and learn from their experiences. It provides children with the opportunity to interact with people of different ethnicities, ages, and abilities, helping them develop a sense of identity, empathy, and belonging. Through participation in multi-generational communities, children are exposed to the life experience, perspective, and social structure that seniors provide, while seniors benefit from the vitality, social connection, and meaning that children bring[7]. The way we plan and design our communities supports the creation of a physical and social environment that can support children as they become active, engaged citizens – or prevent them from doing so.

2   BASIC NEEDS OF CHILDREN

Something as seemingly straightforward as walking through a crowd or boarding a bus looks entirely different when viewed through the eyes of a child. In an effort to consider the unique experiences and perspectives of children, the Bernard van Leer Foundation launched an international project called Urban95, which asks mayors, planners, and designers to consider the city from an elevation of 95 cm – the average height of a three year old child. They ask:

If you could see the city from an elevation of 95 cm, what would you do differently?

Planners, architects, and policy-makers are increasingly beginning to challenge the assumption that a livable built environment for adults also supports the needs of children. Over the past 50 years, concerns about traffic, abductions, and injuries, combined with decreased social connections within local communities, have spurred a culture of protectionism amongst parents and caregivers. As a result, children's access to the city – walking home from school or playing street hockey with friends – has been in decline for decades. According to one study, a number of factors influence children's freedom in their community, including the child's gender, age, proximity of parks, oversight of homes onto public spaces, socioeconomic status of the neighbourhood, and social networks within the community[9]. When children step out of their homes, they are faced with a world that is, at best, indifferent and, at worst, hostile toward them. While the ability for children to explore and engage with their community has been associated with increased self-confidence, independence, resilience, and even increased academic success, children's access to the city is more limited than ever[10]. Children today are granted less access, opportunities, and rights within their communities than their parents, not because the city is disproportionately more dangerous than it was a generation ago, but because the design of our homes, streets, neighbourhoods, and shared spaces supports individual desires over community relationships. The result is a prioritization of cars over people, a lack of community cohesion, and a competition for space[11].

In most municipal planning and design processes, there is lack of planning both for children and with children. The segregation and overregulation of children's activities has resulted in a widespread overshadowing of children's social and developmental needs in favour of discussions around safety and purpose-built environments. Where children are considered as key users of a space, discussions tend to be overwhelmingly focused on the creation of playgrounds, skate parks, schools, and other segregated uses.

Children see and interact with the world differently than adults do, yet their specific spatial, social, and developmental needs are not widely understood, resulting in children being given little consideration when it comes to design. A survey of literature suggests a number of basic needs commonly identified by children and their families with respect to the design and management of their communities. These include:

1. Children need opportunities to join a loose social group of other children without a formal – or prearranged – invitation to play.
2. Children need access to safe, uninhibited outdoor play to support their physical and mental health. Outdoor play should include opportunities to interact with the natural environment – finding bugs, smelling flowers, playing in puddles, or collecting objects – without the need for excessive rules, oversight, or segregation.
3. Children need environments that are safe from traffic, pollution, and undue physical or social hazards, including safe routes to and from school and local playgrounds, allowing them to travel throughout their neighbourhoods safely in order to develop confidence, resilience, and independence.
4. Children need private spaces for themselves and their friends, including tree houses, forts, or clubhouses that are close to home yet away from public view.
5. Children need stable, appropriate, and affordable housing that provides them with private space to rest, study, and play.
6. Children need local access to appropriate early childhood education, child care, and community schools.
7. Children benefit from the opportunity for their parents to work locally.
8. Children benefit from walkable communities, with infrastructure for safe walking, cycling, and recreation.
9. Children benefit from diverse, multi-generational communities, where they can interact with – and learn from – children, adults, and seniors of all races, religions, cultures, and incomes.
10. Children should be given an opportunity to effectively and productively participate in decision-making processes.

This publication explores opportunities for children to be active participants in the design of their communities, thereby supporting the development of an active and engaged society. To limit child-friendly engagement, design, and planning to parks and play spaces is to miss the opportunity for children to actively participate in their environment, and to perpetuate a system where the community is passed down to – rather than co-created with – children. Cities are complex systems that rely on collaborations between multiple departments, agencies, and levels of government for their success. Like all residents, a child's

NATIONAL OCCUPANCY STANDARDS: HOUSING SUITABILITY

The National Occupancy Standards (NOS)[12] define housing suitability based on the required number of bedrooms for a household, as determined by the age, sex, and relationships among household members. An alternative variable, "persons per room," considers all rooms in a private dwelling in relation to the number of household members. While they are not enforced by municipalities, National Occupancy Standards provide a general guideline by which residents, housing providers, and designers can compare and evaluate housing forms and types based on their occupancy.

The NOS defines the number of bedrooms a household requires as follows:

- A maximum of two persons per bedroom.

- Household members, of any age, living as part of a married or common-law couple may share a bedroom with their spouse or common-law partner.

- Parents of any age must have a separate bedroom from their children.

- Single household members 18 years or older should have a separate bedroom.

- Household members under 5 years old of the opposite sex may share a bedroom if doing so would reduce the number of required bedrooms. This situation would arise only in households with an odd number of males under 18, an odd number of females under 18, and at least one female and one male under the age of 5.

- An exception to the above is a household consisting of one individual living alone. Such a household would not need a bedroom (i.e., the individual may live in a studio apartment and be considered to be living in suitable accommodations).

experience of the urban environment extends beyond departmental boundaries and, in the case of schools and public facilities, other levels of government. While the division of responsibilities between governments, departments, and agencies is often imperceptible to the user, the policies and relationships of these partners shape every aspect of a user's experience of the city. By placing children's rights at the forefront of the planning process, local governments and policy-makers can support the development of communities and environments that are accessible, healthy, and livable for all.

FIG. 2.1
CHILDREN'S USE OF PARKS & OPEN SPACE

ENDNOTES

1. United Nations Children's Fund (UNICEF). Building a World Fit for Children. New York: UNICEF, Division of Communication, April 2003. https://www.unicef.org/publications/files/pub_build_wffc_en.pdf (accessed June 2, 2019).

2. Mintzer, Mara. "How Kids Can Help Design Cities." Filmed November 2017. TEDxMileHigh, 14:25. Accessed May 7, 2019. https://www.ted.com/talks/mara_mintzer_how_kids_can_help_design_cities?language=en

3. United Nations Department of Economic and Social Affairs (UN DESA). "68% of the world population projected to live in urban areas by 2050." May 16, 2018. New York: UN DESA. https://www.un.org/development/desa/en/news/population/2018-revision-of-world-urbanization-prospects.html (accessed June 23, 2019).

4. Sharif, Maimunah Mohd. "Foreword." in The City at Eye Level for Kids, edited by Danenberg, Rosa, Vivian Doumpa, and Hans Karssenberg, p.10. Rotterdam: STIPO Publishing, 2018. https://thecityateyelevel.com/app/uploads/2019/06/eBook_CAEL_Kids_Book_Design_Kidsgecomprimeerd.pdf (accessed June 14, 2019).

5. Statistics Canada. 2017. British Columbia [Province] and Canada [Country] (table). Census Profile. 2016 Census. Statistics Canada Catalogue no. 98-316-X2016001. Ottawa. Released November 29, 2017. https://www12.statcan.gc.ca/census-recensement/2016/dp-pd/prof/index.cfm?Lang=E (accessed December 3, 2019).

6. Peñalosa, Enrique. "The Politics of Happiness." Yes!, May 20, 2004. https://www.yesmagazine.org/issues/finding-courage/the-politics-of-happiness (accessed September 25, 2019).

7. Studer, Diana. Put Play to Work: Engaging Children in the Design Process through Play-Based Charrettes. RAIC 690 A&B Syllabus Diploma Project. Victoria, 2018, p. 14.

8. Bernard van Leer Foundation. "Urban95." bernardvanleer.org https://bernardvanleer.org/solutions/urban95/ (accessed May 14, 2019)

9. McAllister, Catherine. "Child Friendly Cities and Land Use Planning: Implications for children's health." Environments Journal. Vol 35 (3): 2008. http://citeseerx.ist.psu.edu/viewdoc/download?doi=10.1.1.393.63&rep=rep1&type=pdf (Accessed November 4, 2019), p. 49.

10. Studer, Diana. Put Play to Work: Engaging Children in the Design Process through Play-Based Charrettes. RAIC 690 A&B Syllabus Diploma Project. Victoria, 2018, p. 14.

11. Patuszyńska, Beata. "Barriers for Warsaw's Youngest Citizens on their Way to School." in The City at Eye Level for Kids, edited by Danenberg, Rosa, Vivian Doumpa, and Hans Karssenberg, p.247. Rotterdam: STIPO Publishing, 2018. https://thecityateyelevel.com/app/uploads/2019/06/eBook_CAEL_Kids_Book_Design_Kidsgecomprimeerd.pdf (accessed June 14, 2019).

12. Canada Mortgage and Housing Corporation. "Housing Standards." Housing in Canada Online. https://cmhc.beyond2020.com/HiCODefinitions_EN.html#_Suitable_dwellings (accessed June 21, 2019).

PART II: POLITICS, POLICY AND THE FUTURE

"What we build teaches those who live in the city, town, or village about our values and concerns."
Richard Register[1]

Children's lives are largely local. As a result, elected officials have the ability to influence children's lives and experiences through the policies they implement, the design ideas they support, and the decisions that they make. The design of housing – and the community in which it is located – can significantly impact how well children and their caregivers are able to navigate, engage with, and benefit from their environments. Child-friendly places recognize that independent play, access, and movement are critical aspects of children's healthy physical and emotional development. The public realm is where children and young people learn about society, where they explore their environment, observe others, and develop a sense of belonging. Giving greater consideration to the creation of child-friendly places can inform the spatial decisions which ensure that attainable, family-friendly housing is available in every community, that schools and core services are co-located within close proximity to

LEGISLATION, REGULATION, AND POLICY

What is the difference between policy, regulation, and legislation? How do they affect the design and development of our shared communities? And who is responsible for developing and enforcing them?

Many municipalities have child and family-friendly policies in place, yet young people often appear to fall off the radar when it comes time to build. Cities and their structures are, too often, designed for the stereotypical, able-bodied adult, overlooking the needs of children, seniors, and people who are living with disabilities. Schools, child care facilities, playgrounds, and other child-friendly amenities have a tendency to lag behind the development of higher-density commercial and residential buildings. As a result, there is often confusion about why a development is permitted when it seemingly does not comply with the residents' vision for their community. Can't municipal policies be enforced? If not, why do cities work so hard to develop them?

There are three interconnected aspects that impact municipal development activities: legislation, regulation, and policy[2]. Legislation refers to a law enacted by a Legislature or other governing body. In Canada, only the provincial and federal governments can pass laws in the form of "legislation". The Province of British Columbia delegates to local governments the ability to create policy and regulation through the Local Government Act and the Community Charter. In other words, the Province is empowered to pass legislation that is applicable throughout the province, while local authorities are empowered to impose policies and regulations that only apply within their respective operating territory and may be unique to each local government. Municipal bylaws, procedures, and regulations must comply with any applicable provincial legislation.

Regulations are rules or directives made and enforced by local authorities, as permitted by legislation. Municipal zoning bylaws, which govern the height, use, and density of a development, are examples of rules that provinces authorize local authorities to enact for application within their specific operating territories. Policy refers to principles, rules, and guidelines formulated or adopted by a municipality to reach its long-term goals. Policy documents, such as Official Community Plans, housing policies, and child and family community policies can help define the overall objectives of a community, but are binding only to the issuing organization itself. In other words, citizens and private developers have no legal obligation to comply with the objectives and guidelines outlined in a policy, provided that they meet all other regulations and legal requirements for development (zoning, building code, etc). If, however, a citizen or developer wishes to propose a change to the regulations for a particular site, for example, rezoning to allow an alternative land use or a change in density, then local government staff is obligated to apply their approved policies to guide the development and application of new regulations for the site. Ideally, policy and regulation will be aligned in order to advance municipal objectives. In reality, however, regulation is not readily altered and often lags behind policy.

residential developments, that safe walking and cycling infrastructure is provided, and that children's well-being is prioritized through building safe, cohesive, and active communities[3]. Children are vulnerable to social and environmental factors due to their age, size, limited experience and developing physical and cognitive abilities. As a result, children's experiences in the built environment often parallel those of other vulnerable populations - women, seniors, and people with disabilities – emphasizing the importance of creating inclusive and supportive environments for all users.

3   PLANNERS' TOOLKIT

As the social, environmental, and economic implications of suburban living have become increasingly clear, the need to infill, densify, and diversify our existing communities has grown. To meet the needs of an ever-expanding population, municipalities across the country are overwhelmingly focusing their policy efforts on mature and urban neighbourhoods, taking advantage of existing infrastructure, transportation networks, and amenities. The recommendations set forth within this publication will, therefore, focus primarily on areas of urban and suburban infill, rather than on greenfield development. This section explores the interrelated policy, regulatory, financial, and procedural tools that local governments can utilize to influence the family-friendliness of their communities and cities as a whole. It will consider the importance of creating child and family-friendly policies that support the development and management of inclusive, multi-generational communities. It will examine the regulatory and financial tools available to support and implement these policies - with a particular focus on supporting the long-term affordability of family-friendly homes - and will outline a number of alternate delivery methods that are available to local governments seeking to incentivize predetermined development, tenancy, and affordability targets. Finally, this section will investigate the impact of the aforementioned tools on the financial feasibility of new residential development projects.

The best future for children is shaped by the stability of their homes, families, and communities. Access to appropriate housing, quality schools, safe communities, and healthy natural environments are all critical contributors to healthy child development. Developing inclusive communities that meet the needs of a broad and varied population is a complex undertaking that requires considerable study, investment, and collaboration over time. It is not enough to provide critical, family-friendly housing and amenities after there is urgent need for them; these services and facilities must be in place from the outset to create stable, viable, and complete multi-generational communities. To support a diverse, multi-generational range of urban residents – from children to seniors – it is therefore necessary to implement a complete, whole-of-government approach that acknowledges the interrelationships between housing, child care, education, employment, transportation, and recreation. The most promising policy and regulatory approaches are those interventions that cross disciplinary and departmental boundaries and provide whole-of-life benefits and opportunities for multiple generations, family-types, and household compositions. Municipal policies, regulations, financial measures, and planning processes can work together to help local governments incrementally shape development and pave the way for families to thrive in their communities[4].

Practices	Direct Cost			Benefit		
	Low	Medium	High	Rural	Suburban	Urban
Policy Measures						
Official Community Plans and Neighbourhood Plans		■		med	med-high	high
Missing Middle Policy	■			low	high	high
Secondary Suites Policies and Programs	■			low	med	med
Housing First Policies for Surplus Public Land	■			med	high	high
Child and Youth Consultation Policy		■		med-high	med-high	med-high
Full Spectrum CPTED Policy		■		low-med	med-high	high
Regulatory Measures						
Missing Middle Zoning	■			low	high	high
Inclusionary Zoning	■			low	med-high	med-high
Performance Zoning		■		low	med	med-high
Density Bonusing	■			low	med-high	high
Residential Rental Tenure Bylaw	■			low	med-high	high
Financial Measures						
Development Levies and Fee Waivers		■		low	med	high
Property Tax Exemptions		■		med	high	high
Municipal Land Banks			■	low-med	med-high	med-high
Partnering Policy with Investment		■		med-high	high	high
Partnerships and Alternative Delivery Methods						
Fast Tracking the Development Approval Process		■		low	med	med-high
Housing Agreements	■			med	high	high
Municipal Children's Advocate			■	med-high	high	high
Support Capacity within the Non-Profit Housing Sector		■		high	high	high

FIG. 3.1 MUNICIPAL COST-BENEFIT OF SELECTED POLICIES AND REGULATORY MEASURES

Direct Cost:
Low: can be absorbed into regular staff capacity and operating budgets
Medium: may require additional staff capacity and may have short-term budget implications
High: may require significant and ongoing investment

Benefit:
Low: will likely have minimal impact on the composition of a community
Medium: some impact, but overall community change will require additional time and investment
High: significant potential to quickly alter the composition of a community

4 POLICY MEASURES

Local governments can have a direct and significant impact on the location of child and family-friendly services and amenities, the creation of active, walkable and transit-oriented communities, and quality of life through their municipal planning and regulatory processes. Policy drives and directs investment, shapes decision-making, and provides a framework for discussions about the future of a community. As a result, policies that consider children in the built environment hold enormous potential for helping a municipality meet the needs of children, their families, and – indeed – all residents in a comprehensive, holistic manner.

Official Community Plans (OCPs) and Neighbourhood Plans
Official Community Plans (OCPs) hold significant potential in shaping child and family-friendly communities by outlining types, locations, and proximities of land uses within a municipality. An Official Community Plan (OCP) describes the long term vision of the community and guides the decisions of elected officials and local government staff, particularly in cases where lands are being rezoned or developed outside "as-of-right" permissions.

By their nature, OCPs have the potential for broad and intersectional impact, providing guidance on matters including housing density and diversity, transportation infrastructure, public space, and local employment. The incorporation of family-friendly policy wording has the potential to influence housing form and affordability, particularly when paired with investment and enforced through regulation. In order to capitalize on the potential of OCPs to effectively shape a community, local governments must encourage ongoing partnerships with other departments, agencies, and levels of governments while maintaining a strong understanding of the financial implications of local policies, regulations, incentives, and investments as they relate to development outcomes, affordability, and social benefits.

Advantages	Challenges
<ul><li>OCPs allow municipalities to align future development with investments in transit, infrastructure, public amenities, and schools.</li><li>OCPs can promote revitalization, resilience, and placemaking by considering the broader impact of a mix of land uses and supporting the pre-zoning of lands for future development.</li><li>Municipalities are required to maintain current OCPs under the Local Government Act, thereby providing the opportunity to continually re-evaluate the needs, demographics, and challenges of local families.</li><li>Can be used to encourage duplex, town/row housing, walk-up apartments, and other missing middle housing forms across a broad range of communities.</li><li>Can enable municipalities to provide grants and loans to targeted areas of the community in order to stimulate private sector investment.</li></ul>	<ul><li>May require the creation and management of phased development agreements to ensure that family-friendly services and amenities are provided in a timely fashion alongside housing.</li><li>Often requires additional municipal or provincial investment to fully realize OCP objectives.</li><li>Political and financial barriers may emerge during the implementation of OCP policies and objectives.</li><li>Children are often excluded from the consultation process and may need to be actively sought out and engaged. Municipalities may need to train staff on engagement strategies to effectively gather input from children and their caregivers.</li></ul>

Legislative References

Local Government Act, RSBC. 2015, c-1: Part 14: Planning and Land Use Management, Division 1: General

Local Government Act, RSBC. 2015, c-1: Part 14: Planning and Land Use Management, Division 4: Official Community Plans

Local Government Act, RSBC. 2015, c-1: Part 14: Planning and Land Use Management, Division 5: Zoning Bylaws

Local Government Act, RSBC. 2015, c-1: Part 14: Planning and Land Use Management, Division 6: Development Approval Information Requirements

Local Government Act, RSBC. 2015, c-1: Part 14: Planning and Land Use Management, Division 12: Phased Development Agreements, Section 516: Phased Development Agreements

Local Government Act, RSBC. 2015, c-1: Part 14: Planning and Land Use Management, Division 19: Development Costs Recovery, Section 565: Deductions from Development Cost Charges

Missing Middle Policy

A central tenet of most Official Community Plans and municipal housing policies is the provision of an appropriate range and mix of housing types, tenures, and densities to meet the current and future needs of residents. The term "missing middle" is often used to describe a range of housing types that are compatible with the character and scale of single-detached neighbourhoods. Missing middle housing – which includes multiplexes, courtyard housing, row houses, townhouses, and walk-up apartment buildings – is an attempt to diversify the housing stock in urban and suburban communities. This type of housing may promote walkability, capitalize on existing infrastructure, and promote affordability in existing communities.

Missing middle housing is gaining prominence in discussions about densification, complete communities, and housing affordability. The development of missing middle policies – which often address the needs of families from the outset – may help to increase the stock of family-friendly housing and allow municipalities to address the needs of a growing number of urban families over time.

Advantages	Challenges
• Strong policy frameworks can help streamline the development approval process, allowing housing to be constructed with greater efficiency. • Missing middle policies can encourage densification and diversification, including duplex, town/row housing and other family-friendly housing forms, across broad community areas, rather than on a site-by-site basis.	• Likely requires the development of design guidelines for missing middle housing to educate builders and residents about medium-density design options and standards. • Children and their families will likely need to be actively sought out and engaged during the consultation process.

Advantages (cont.)	Challenges (cont.)
<ul><li>Allows municipalities to co-locate residential development in areas with upcoming investment in transit, infrastructure, amenities, and schools.</li><li>Community opposition is addressed at the outset rather than on a site-by-site basis.</li><li>Enabling policies can allow municipalities to provide grants and loans that incentivize family-friendly housing developments and subsidize the cost of homes for low-income families.</li><li>Missing middle policies support infill housing, while providing enough density to support investment in schools, public facilities, and local services.</li></ul>	<ul><li>May require the creation of housing agreements or additional support from other levels of government, housing providers, or non-profit partners to ensure that a portion of new missing middle homes remain available to a broad range of families.</li><li>Lower density missing middle housing may not be financially-feasible for developers to build, particularly in areas with high land costs.</li><li>May require municipal incentives in the form of tax exemptions, fee waivers, and fast-tracked applications to make missing middle housing forms more appealing to developers.</li></ul>

Legislative References

Local Government Act, RSBC. 2015, c-1: Part 14: Planning and Land Use Management, Division 5: Zoning Bylaws

Local Government Act, RSBC. 2015, c-1: Part 14: Planning and Land Use Management, Division 7: Development Permits, Section 488: Designation of Development Permit Areas

Local Government Act, RSBC. 2015, c-1: Part 14: Planning and Land Use Management, Division 11: Subdivision and Development

Land Title Act, RSBC. 1996, c-250: Division 2: Subdivision of Land

Strata Property Act, SBC. 1998, c-43: Part 5: Property

Secondary Suites Policies and Programs

Supporting secondary suites, including lock-off, garden and laneway suites, is a cost-effective way to integrate and increase the supply of rental housing throughout a broad range of new and existing communities. Secondary suites can both assist owners with mortgage and property costs and help alleviate housing affordability and availability concerns for a wide range of residents. These units can provide families with the opportunity to live in a home with access to a private or semi-private outdoor space – either as tenants or as owners with a mortgage-helper - in neighbourhoods where this may not otherwise be an option. Through secondary suites policies and programs, municipalities have the opportunity to support property owners as they develop and maintain secondary rental housing on existing properties. Municipalities may have the opportunity to support family-friendly secondary suites in areas with high demand through loans, grants, or other incentives as defined by their secondary suites policy.

Advantages	Challenges
• Secondary suites can provide a solution to the demand for family-friendly rental housing, while assisting homeowners with the cost of purchasing and maintaining their home.	• Secondary suites are often developed and managed illegally - even in areas where they are permitted - because it can be time-consuming and expensive to bring existing units up to current fire and building code standards.
• Secondary suites require minimal investment from local governments, with the exception of building safety inspections, development application and permit reviews, and public education campaigns.	• There can be strong opposition to legalizing secondary suites from local residents due to anticipated impacts on parking and community character.
• Secondary suites may enable families to live in homes with access to a shared backyard or garden area, which may otherwise be unavailable to them.	• Secondary suites are often smaller than the principal dwelling and may not be appropriate for all family types.

Advantages (cont.)	Challenges (cont.)
• In mature neighbourhoods, where little infill or rental housing is being built, secondary suites provide a cost-effective way of addressing affordability needs for both homeowners and tenants, while also supporting housing densification. • In rural areas and mature neighbourhoods with large proportions of single-family houses on large lots, secondary suites can be easily incorporated into the existing community fabric without significantly altering the existing character of the community.	• Some homeowners may be reluctant to rent a suite in their home or on their property due to restrictions under the Residential Tenancy Act and may be reluctant to rent to families with children because of concerns about noise, safety, and privacy. • Secondary suites are often intended to maximize revenue and support income for the homeowner, therefore these units may not be broadly affordable for families. • It can be cost prohibitive for building owners to upgrade suites to meet the building code and obtain a permit, therefore some owners will choose to operate secondary suites illegally.

Legislative References

Local Government Act, RSBC. 2015, c-1: Part 14: Planning and Land Use Management, Division 5: Zoning Bylaws, Section 481.1: Residential Rental Tenure

Local Government Act, RSBC. 2015, c-1: Part 14: Planning and Land Use Management, Division 5: Zoning Bylaws, Section 479: Zoning Bylaws

Local Government Act, RSBC. 2015, c-1: Part 14: Planning and Land Use Management, Division 7: Development Permits, Section 488: Designation of Development Permit Areas

Community Charter, SBC. 2003, c-26: Part 5: Municipal Government and Procedures, Division 3: Bylaw Procedures, Section 140: Revision of Bylaws

Strata Property Act, SBC. 1998, c-43: Part 8: Rentals

Housing First Policies for Surplus Public Land

Repurposing surplus land owned by governments, school boards, or other public agencies provides an efficient way of acquiring land for affordable housing in an otherwise cost-prohibitive market. In some municipalities, housing first policies have been developed for surplus public land, which earmarks decommissioned lands for the development of affordable housing on a long-term lease basis. These housing first policies could be expanded to include requirements for larger, family-sized homes across a range of missing middle housing forms to help address the affordable housing needs of families. However, because the presence of local schools and early childhood education and care services are integral components of family-friendly communities, policies reallocating surplus school lands should ensure that the educational needs of existing and future residents can be met through existing and planned neighbourhood school capacities.

Advantages	Challenges
• Repurposing surplus land is an effective way of moderating development costs, particularly where base land costs are prohibitive, thereby supporting the affordability of housing in a community. • When structured as a long-term lease, the municipality retains ownership of the land and, therefore, has the ability to define housing forms and tenure types and protect the affordability of the housing development over time.	• Decommissioned land may not be in an ideal location for family-friendly or affordable housing (e.g. not close to schools, transit, or services). • Care must be taken to ensure that schools and early childhood educational and care facilities are provided close to intensified housing developments, particularly if the intent is to increase the density of family-friendly housing in a community.

Advantages (cont.)	Challenges (cont.)
• Repurposing surplus lands requires minimal additional investment from local governments, but offers significant benefits in terms of affordable housing. • Municipalities have the ability to require the provision of family-friendly homes and align development with investment in schools, public facilities, and transit infrastructure.	• Appropriate safeguards must be put in place to ensure that housing built on surplus land remains affordable for the long-term. • In a long-term lease arrangement, developers and landlords do not benefit from gains in land value. Additional incentives may be required to find a suitable developer or partner. • Some lenders may be hesitant to finance developments on leasehold land because they have less security in the event of a loan default. • Land contamination on surplus land can be a concern and land can be costly to remediate.

Legislative References

Local Government Act, RSBC. 2015, c-1: Part 14: Planning and Land Use Management, Division 7: Development Permits, Section 488: Designation of Development Permit Areas

Local Government Act, RSBC. 2015, c-1: Part 14: Planning and Land Use Management, Division 20: School Site Acquisition Charges, Section 479: Zoning Bylaws

Community Charter, SBC. 2003, c-26: Part 5: Municipal Government and Procedures, Division 3: Bylaw Procedures, Section 140: Revision of Bylaws

Strata Property Act, SBC. 1998, c-43: Part 8: Rentals

Child and Youth Consultation Policy

To create child-friendly places, it is necessary to effectively consult with children and youth throughout the planning process. When decision-makers engage with children, listen to their ideas, and understand their specific social and spatial needs, it can help inform and strengthen decision-making and contribute to a more inclusive and supportive built environment. While children and youth are rarely intentionally excluded from the consultation process, additional efforts may be required to seek out their input and involve them in the planning process. This may include adapting the location, format, or process for consultations and engagement, providing child care for caregivers, or ensuring that events take place outside of school hours. For more information about consulting with children and youth, refer to Part 4: Participatory Planning with Children.

Advantages	Challenges
• Targeting consultation activities helps municipalities consider the needs of children, youth, and caregivers. • Children frequently consider the relationships between people, animals, insects, water, and nature when talking about their environments, elements which are often overlooked during planning and development processes. • Including children and youth in the planning and engagement process empowers and prepares them to become and remain active and engaged citizens.	• Many adults undervalue children's opinions and believe that children cannot articulate or advocate for their own needs. • Consultation with children is often limited to play-based learning opportunities and not true engagement activities. • Facilitators may require additional training to understand the social and developmental needs of children and how to effectively engage with a variety of age groups. • Some people fear that children's demands may be unreasonable and result in "wasting" the time of municipal staff and consultants.

Advantages (cont.)	Challenges (cont.)
• Children tend to prioritize play, collaboration, and social interaction in their discussions about the built environment and they are often more accepting of others, regardless of race, culture, religion, gender, or socio-economic backgrounds. • Children, especially young children, are vulnerable due to their size, age, and experience in urban environments. Their limited independent mobility draws attention to the accessibility and safety of streets, sidewalks, bicycle infrastructure, and other public amenities. Considering children's needs can have positive impacts on accessibility and inclusivity for all residents.	

Legislative References

Local Government Act, RSBC. 2015, c-1: Part 14: Planning and Land Use Management, Division 4: Official Community Plans, Section 475: Consultation During Development of Official Community Plan

Community Charter, SBC. 2003, c-26: Part 5: Municipal Government and Procedures, Division 4 — Committees, Commissions and Other Bodies

Full Spectrum CPTED Policy

To create a community that is appropriate for children, municipalities must first support the development of a community that is safe for children. Crime Prevention Through Environmental Design (CPTED) techniques have been utilized in the design of the built environment for nearly four decades. Based on the principles of defensible space – natural surveillance, access control, territoriality, and maintenance – early Crime Prevention Through Environmental Design (CPTED) methods sought to reduce or eliminate criminal behaviour through modification of the built environment. Second Generation CPTED - or Full Spectrum Crime Prevention Through Environment Design – combines placemaking, restorative practices, compassionate enquiry, arts for social change, and peace building methodologies in order to address community safety, reduce crime, embrace culture, and support social connection. Local governments hoping to develop and support safe, integrated, and inclusive communities should consider creating a Full Spectrum CPTED policy that is broadly applied across all developments and is supported by an on-staff CPTED professional. The CPTED professional should be involved in developing and reviewing all municipal plans, policies, major residential development applications, transportation and infrastructure strategies, and public space designs, thereby helping to create and maintain safe, cohesive, and vibrant communities for residents of all ages.

Advantages	Challenges
• Full Spectrum CPTED supports community safety, cohesion, cultural expression, and vibrancy for residents of all ages.	• Most local governments and planning professionals have a limited understanding of CPTED principles.
• Safety is a critical component of any community, but is of particular concern for children and other vulnerable populations.	• First Generation CPTED principles can impact people's behaviour in a space, however they do little to create or enhance feelings of community.

Advantages (cont.)	Challenges (cont.)
• Well-considered CPTED approaches can reduce the need for ongoing public spending on policing, vandalism, surveillance, and security. • The presence of a CPTED professional on staff ensures that safety, comfort, and community cohesion are considered from the outset in every major development, policy, and initiative.	• If applied incorrectly, CPTED principles can create environments that are hostile for children and other vulnerable populations. • All CPTED interventions must continually consider impacts on racialized, minority, and other vulnerable populations to ensure that they are not negatively impacted or targeted by these policies.

Legislative References

Local Government Act, RSBC. 2015, c-1: Part 14: Planning and Land Use Management, Division 4: Official Community Plans, Section 474: Policy Statements that may be Included

Community Charter, SBC. 2003, c-26: Part 5: Municipal Government and Procedures, Division 4 — Committees, Commissions and Other Bodies

5   REGULATORY MEASURES

If the child-friendliness of the built environment is measured, in part, by how livable and inclusive it is, then municipalities have the potential to develop enabling regulations as an effective means of influencing the character, composition, and configuration of a particular area. Through municipal zoning bylaws, local governments regulate and enforce matters relating land use, proximity, massing, building orientation, and density. Likewise, municipalities are able to align regulations with investment in order to address the current and future needs of residents and users of a particular community. For example, family-friendly housing should be co-located close to schools, public facilities, employment uses, and transit stops at densities that can adequately support each of these services and facilities. Generally speaking, the closer housing is to schools, early child care and education facilities, services, amenities, and transit, the more likely it is that children and their families will feel supported – and be able to thrive - within that community.

Many families are finding themselves increasingly priced out of many of BC's communities, particularly those close to schools, public facilities, and urban centres. Due to the fact that housing affordability is a key barrier to many families, several of the tools in this section focus on supporting and maintaining housing affordability in both existing and emerging communities.

Missing Middle Zoning

Missing middle housing forms are those that exist between low-density, single detached homes and high-density apartment buildings and which can be easily integrated into the fabric of most existing residential communities without significantly altering the character of the neighbourhood. This type of gentle density can help address the housing needs of families in both new and existing communities and includes multiplexes, townhouses, row houses, courtyard housing, and walk-up apartments.

Local governments have the opportunity to influence the creation of a more supportive regulatory environment for affordable, family-friendly housing by pre-zoning broad areas of land through overlays or updates to the municipal zoning bylaw. A number of spatial and land use characteristics associated with family-friendly communities and housing affordability can be promoted through pre-designating and pre-zoning lands to permit a range of missing middle housing types, including allowing higher densities, more compact or infill development, reduced lot frontages sizes, and co-locating housing around schools, employment uses, and transit centres. To be fully effective, however, the design of missing middle housing forms may need to be codified through design-based regulations and standards. At a minimum, local governments should develop design guidelines for medium-density and multi-family residential housing forms to educate and inform builders, developers, investors, and residents about missing middle housing design options and standards.

Advantages	Challenges
• The development industry often supports pre-zoning of lands because it can help streamline the development approval process, thus allowing housing to be constructed with greater efficiency, while decreasing developer risk.	• The development of missing middle zoning overlays can require considerable resources upfront, particularly in communities with significant opposition.

Advantages (cont.)	Challenges (cont.)
• Can reduce inequity by allowing densification and diversification of missing middle housing forms across broad community areas rather than on a site-by-site basis. • Pre-zoning can allow municipalities to align future development with investments in transit, infrastructure, public facilities and amenities, and schools. • Community opposition to increased density is addressed at the outset rather than on a site-by-site basis. • Pre-zoning can help municipalities incentivize missing middle housing forms that can accommodate the needs of families.	• Pre-zoning may limit a municipality's ability to seek community amenity contributions as part of the development approval process. • Likely requires the development of missing middle design guidelines to educate builders and residents about family-friendly housing options and design standards. • Pre-zoning for higher density may increase the value of land, making it more expensive to purchase and develop. This type of up-zoning may make it more difficult to achieve overall affordability targets. • Infill development may not provide enough density to address climate change.

Legislative References

Local Government Act, RSBC. 2015, c-1: Part 14: Planning and Land Use Management, Division 5: Zoning Bylaws

Local Government Act, RSBC. 2015, c-1: Part 14: Planning and Land Use Management, Division 7: Development Permits, Section 488: Designation of Development Permit Areas

Local Government Act, RSBC. 2015, c-1: Part 14: Planning and Land Use Management, Division 11: Subdivision and Development

Land Title Act, RSBC. 1996, c-250: Division 2: Subdivision of Land

Strata Property Act, SBC. 1998, c-43: Part 5: Property

Inclusionary Zoning

Inclusionary zoning is the most frequently cited regulatory tool used to support the creation of affordable housing. Inclusionary zoning refers to municipal zoning practices that require developers to provide a portion of newly-constructed affordable housing units or to provide a financial contribution to a municipal affordable housing fund. Local governments in British Columbia are permitted to implement voluntary inclusionary zoning programs - often paired with density-bonusing tools - however, provincial legislation in British Columbia does not provide express authority to implement mandatory inclusionary zoning programs. When applied alongside other tools and incentives, voluntary inclusionary zoning may help municipalities achieve overall affordable housing targets in a broad range of communities. To support family-friendly housing development objectives, local governments may offer incentives in the form of density bonuses, application fee waivers, tax deferrals, or fast-tracked approvals in exchange for affordable housing units.

Advantages	Challenges
• Inclusionary zoning has been proven to produce affordable homes in markets where such housing would not normally have been developed. • If inclusionary zoning contributions are aligned with requirements for larger, family-friendly homes, there is potential to increase the supply of housing that is both affordable and suitable.	• Local governments in British Columbia do not currently have the express authority to implement mandatory inclusionary zoning programs and must rely on density bonusing, tax exemptions, fee waivers, and housing agreements to fulfill the objectives of an inclusionary zoning-based program. • The application of inclusionary zoning is often limited to large-scale, multi-unit residential developments.

Advantages (cont.)	Challenges (cont.)
• Inclusionary zoning is relatively inexpensive for municipalities to implement and can be paired with design-based incentives to influence the form and type of homes developed. • Inclusionary zoning helps to avoid project-specific, local opposition to affordable housing by integrating affordable housing units across a wide spectrum of developments and communities. • Municipalities can tailor voluntary inclusionary zoning programs to meet the housing objectives and targets that are outlined in their Official Community Plans.	• Density bonuses for voluntary participation are most beneficial in high-growth areas where land values are high and increased density is a significant asset. • Some argue that inclusionary zoning may be seen to unfairly target new developments, resulting in lower quality units or encouraging cash-in-lieu contributions instead of the construction of new units.

Legislative References

Local Government Act, RSBC. 2015, c-1: Part 14: Planning and Land Use Management, Division 5: Zoning Bylaws, Section 482: Density Benefits for Amenities, Affordable Housing and Special Needs Housing

Community Charter, SBC. 2003, c-26: Division 3: Bylaw Procedures, Section 140: Revision of Bylaws

Performance Zoning

Performance zoning is an alternative zoning practice that regulates the design and location of land use based on the characteristics of a particular site and its ability to support development. Municipalities using this approach may replace conventional zoning with form-based or performance criteria to increase the range of uses, building types, and carrying capacity of a site. It allows planners to encourage certain building forms – such as missing middle housing – and create places that consider the employment, cultural, residential, and recreational needs of users by setting outcome targets and allowing design and land use to be adapted to meet these targets. A number of Canadian municipalities are beginning to adopt some of the key principles of performance based regulations in their zoning bylaws[5].

Advantages	Challenges
• Performance zoning is most effective in suburban, brownfield, and transitional areas where redevelopment has been stalled by conventional zoning practices. • Performance zoning allows municipalities to leverage existing infrastructure, support a wider range of land uses, protect the natural environment, and encourage development projects that meet a municipality's broader community objectives. • Performance zoning allows for a broader mix of land uses, supporting livable, walkable, and active community life by allowing for a mix of residential, employment, and service uses.	• Performance zoning often requires a complete alteration of a municipality's land use policies and regulations. As a result, performance zoning may be appropriate only for designated areas with high environmental or contextual sensitivity. • Managing, evaluating, and revising performance zoning requires more technical expertise, staff time, and administrative costs than conventional zoning. • Local residents may be resistant to new developments in their community, particularly if they differ in use or character from other developments in the area.

Advantages (cont.)	Challenges (cont.)
• Performance zoning can encourage the creation of family-friendly affordable housing building types through opportunities for increased density, diversity of housing types, and other design innovations.	• Performance zoning is less effective when applied to small parcels or to minor land development proposals.

Legislative References

Local Government Act, RSBC. 2015, c-1: Part 14: Planning and Land Use Management, Division 5: Zoning Bylaws

Local Government Act, RSBC. 2015, c-1: Part 14: Planning and Land Use Management, Division 7: Development Permits, Section 488: Designation of Development Permit Areas

Local Government Act, RSBC. 2015, c-1: Part 14: Planning and Land Use Management, Division 4: Official Community Plans, Section 473: Content and Process Requirements

Community Charter, SBC. 2003, c-26: Division 3: Bylaw Procedures, Section 140: Revision of Bylaws

Density Bonusing

The *Local Government Act* allows municipalities to grant height and density increases in exchange for the provision of certain features or amenities that benefit the overall community and meet municipal objectives. Density bonusing provisions are generally defined in a municipality's zoning bylaw and may also be supported through the creation of additional, community-specific density bonusing policies. A density bonus model is a voluntary mechanism through which developers may provide an amenity - such as higher bedroom counts, affordable housing units, or energy efficient building features - or a community amenity contribution in exchange for an increase in density. Developers often have the option of providing the municipality with a predetermined financial contribution that is earmarked for a specific public use. Municipalities have the opportunity to modify density bonusing programs to incentivize family-friendly homes with higher bedroom counts by subtracting the third bedroom of units from FAR calculations or by increasing FAR allowances for specific housing or unit types, provided any increase in building size will not negatively impact the surrounding environment or infrastructure. As a voluntary program, developers have the option to develop to the permitted as-of-right base density with no additional contributions required.

Advantages	Challenges
• Density bonusing can encourage the development of a substantial number of larger, family-friendly and/or affordable housing units, particularly when applied to larger mixed-use or multi-unit residential projects. • Once established, density bonusing programs require minimal staff involvement or municipal investment.	• Density bonusing is effective only where developers are interested in achieving higher densities, such as in urban centres, large multi-unit or mixed-use projects, or expanding markets. • Implementation may be challenged for giving too much density to developers in exchange for too little public benefit. This is a particular risk when developers offer financial or off-site contributions.

Advantages (cont.)	Challenges (cont.)
• Density bonusing can be used to achieve OCP density targets by encouraging an intensification of missing middle and family-friendly housing development in urban areas, walkable communities, school zones, and those communities that are well-serviced by public transit. • As a voluntary program, municipalities have the ability to request specific family-friendly amenities and features in return for added density, as defined by their approved policies.	• Most municipalities offer density bonusing for affordable housing and may be reluctant to add increased bedroom counts or amenity requirements for fear of decreased uptake. This concern can be addressed by requiring that municipal affordability targets be met first, and then allowing additional density (up to a defined maximum) for family-friendly features. • Density bonusing can be complex and its implications are often not well understood.

Legislative References
Local Government Act, RSBC. 2015, c-1: Division 5: Zoning Bylaws, Section 482: Density Benefits for Amenities, Affordable Housing and Special Needs Housing

Community Charter, SBC. 2003, c-26: Division 3: Bylaw Procedures, Section 140: Revision of Bylaws

Residential Rental Tenure Bylaw

Residential rental tenure bylaws acknowledge that rental housing remains the most feasible option for many families. The majority of British Columbia's purpose-built rental stock was constructed between 1960 and 1980, therefore, many buildings are now approaching the end of their useful life and may be in need of significant maintenance or repair. Historically, these units were often designed with a larger floor area, making them prime candidates for conversion to privately-owned condominiums. Due to the overall lack of family-sized units available, families are disproportionately impacted when an existing unit is lost to demolition or conversion. Given the lack of developable land in many communities across the province, the preservation of existing affordable housing stock will become an increasingly important component of many municipal housing strategies.

Local governments may enact residential rental tenure zoning bylaws to prohibit and regulate the demolition of residential rental properties in multi-family developments and the conversion of such properties to a purpose other than residential rental[6]. When combined with other land use tools, including density bonusing and housing agreements, local governments have the ability to support the creation and maintenance of family-friendly rental housing in both mature and emerging areas.

Advantages	Challenges
• It is usually less expensive to maintain existing residential rental properties than it is to construct new buildings. • Demolition controls can be used to support the preservation and adaptive reuse of historic buildings if coupled with preservation programs and incentives.	• In some cases, upgrading rental housing may result in rent increases. Housing agreements, grants, rent supplements, and partnerships may be needed to address any change in affordability of these units.

Advantages (cont.)	Challenges (cont.)
- Can help preserve larger, existing rental units that would otherwise be demolished or converted to condominiums. - Recognizes the importance of rental housing for a wide variety of tenants – including families – as a viable and sustainable housing model. - As an approving authority, Councils have the ability to prevent conversions on any existing occupied, stratified buildings during a change in occupancy.	- Partnerships with provincial governments and non-profit housing agencies may be required to protect tenants from the negative impacts of renovation and redevelopment. - A rental preservation policy may be politically unpalatable and may anger property owners and developers if it applies to privately held property.

Legislative References

Local Government Act, RSBC. 2015, c-1: Part 14: Planning and Land Use Management, Division 5: Zoning Bylaws, Section 481.1: Residential Rental Tenure

Strata Property Act, SBC. 1998, c-43: Part 8: Rentals

6 FINANCIAL MEASURES

By leveraging local planning processes and tools, municipalities may have a significant impact on the financial viability of family-friendly housing forms and, potentially, on whether any cost savings may be able to passed on to buyers. If planners are fully aware of the financial implications of the tools and processes available to them – from rezoning and density bonusing to fee waivers and fast-tracked application processes – then it becomes possible to support developers' business interests, while simultaneously fulfilling municipal objectives for more diverse and affordable housing stock, improved public amenities, and enhanced livability without significant outright municipal investment[7].

Development Levies and Fee Waivers

Development levies, often referred to as "exactions," are tools that allow fees to be levied on developments. When fees are waived or adjusted in exchange for affordable housing, they are often referred to as "reverse exactions." "Linkage fees," are development levies that are linked to employment-generating uses and are calculated based on the demand for affordable housing that a commercial development will create in the future. As a condition of development approval, development levies are paid by developers into a municipal fund that is dedicated to building and supporting affordable housing in the community. Most local governments give the developer the option of building affordable housing units themselves in lieu of paying the fees. This approach has the advantage of incorporating housing into a diverse range of community types and locations. Local governments may apply development levies and fee waivers alone or in combination with other tools in order to incentivize family-friendly development.

Advantages	Challenges
• Linkage fees support the creation and rehabilitation of affordable housing close to employment uses, which benefits residents of all ages.	• Development levies may raise base market housing prices as developers attempt to recuperate their expenses by passing these costs on to buyers.

Advantages (cont.)	Challenges (cont.)
• Development levies are generally paid into a municipally-managed fund. When a municipality uses these funds to develop affordable housing, they have the ability to create family-sized and missing middle housing types to serve the needs of local families. • Waiving or adjusting development levies in exchange for affordable or family-friendly housing allows the developer to recover costs and profit loss from compliance, while meeting municipal objectives. • Development levies are most effective in urban centres that are experiencing sustained growth. Careful negotiation may be required to promote the development of units that are suitable for families.	• Development levies tend to encourage smaller, intrinsically more affordable, residential developments that are more suited to individuals than to families. • Municipalities instituting development levies must be knowledgeable about the real estate market and be prepared to continually evaluate, amend, and suspend these levies if they begin to have a negative impact on the overall local economy. • There is some debate as to whether local governments have the legal authority to apply development levies and fee waivers.

Legislative References

Local Government Act, RSBC. 2015, c-1: Part 14: Planning and Land Use Management, Division 19: Development Costs Recovery, Section 563: Development for which Charges may be Waived or Reduced

Community Charter, SBC. 2003, c-26.: Division 2: Fees, Section 194: Municipal Fees

Property Tax Exemptions

Local governments have the ability to support the development of more affordable, family-friendly housing in a community through tax exemption policies. Tax exemptions can be applied to the value of land, the building, or both. Once all conditions of the housing agreement have been met, municipalities can exempt the property from taxation for a predetermined period of time. Local governments may choose to limit the scope of tax exemptions or elect to cap the total amount of tax revenue they are willing to forego in any one year. Tax exemptions can be paired with family-friendly housing policies and targets to encourage the construction or long-term preservation of affordable, family-friendly rental housing.

Advantages	Challenges
• Tax exemptions can be used to incentivize larger, family-friendly units or missing middle housing forms in a broad range of communities, particularly when family-friendly housing policies are in place. • Waiving or adjusting property taxes allows the developer to reduce and recover losses incurred by providing affordable housing units. • High land costs are making it more difficult to ensure new projects are financially-viable. Tax exemptions may help incentivize certain housing types, while preserving affordability on high-value parcels of land.	• Housing agreements must be drafted and managed over time to ensure long-term affordability. • Investors may be concerned that housing agreements will not allow rents to keep pace with market growth or with increasing operating and maintenance costs. • Property tax exemptions may not be enough to substantially cover a developer's losses in profit.

Legislative References

Local Government Act, RSBC. 2015, c-1: Part 14: Planning and Land Use Management, Division 2: Responsibilities, Procedures and Authorities, Section 462: Fees related to Applications and Inspections

Local Government Act, RSBC. 2015, c-1: Part 14: Planning and Land Use Management, Division 4: Tax Rates and Exemptions, Section 396: Tax Exemptions Under Partnering Agreement

Community Charter, SBC. 2003, c-26.: Division 7: Permissive Exemptions, Section 226: Revitalization Tax Exemptions

Municipal Land Banks

Municipalities occasionally have the opportunity to acquire land through a first right of refusal, annexed or surplus government lands, donated lands, or, occasionally, via abandoned or foreclosed properties. While municipalities have the option to purchase land on the open market, land prices in British Columbia have been steadily increasing over the years, therefore this method of purchasing land would require a significant investment that would likely outweigh any benefits gained. For key sites with high urban or contextual sensitivity, other policy and regulatory tools would be more appropriate to incentivize the development of affordable, family-friendly housing and amenities.

Advantages	Challenges
• Can support redevelopment on vacant and abandoned lots, resulting in increased property tax revenues and the strategic development of housing that meets municipal objectives. • Reduces the cost of land associated with development, allowing larger, less profitable units to be constructed, which may meet the needs of local families. • The municipality maintains control over the future development of land in key areas.	• Municipalities may lack sufficient funds to acquire new land, particularly in areas of rapid development. • Development may require ongoing and effective coordination between the land bank, the City, developers, and other levels of government. • May be difficult to make projects financially-viable if developers are not able to benefit from increases in land value over time.

Legislative References

Community Charter, SBC. 2003, c-26.: Part 6: Financial Management, Division 3: Expenditures, Liabilities and Investments, Section 184: Property Accepted in Trust

Partnering Policy with Investment

Local governments have a unique opportunity to develop partnerships with other agencies and levels of government in order to align investment to achieve desirable municipal policy outcomes. By aligning family-friendly housing with broader amenity and infrastructure investments, local governments are able to address affordability, livability, and economic viability in areas experiencing revitalization and investment.

This approach may have a significant impact on families when paired with investment in schools, child care facilities, and public transit networks. Supporting families in walkable, amenity-rich communities is key to creating healthy and inclusive communities. Furthermore, ensuring that family-friendly housing is located near rapid bus or transit lines is a critical component of reducing household costs and increasing affordability, while supporting the independent mobility of residents of all ages, including children, youth, and seniors. To facilitate more integrated planning, regional coordination between government agencies – including school boards, regional transportation providers, and social agencies – and community stakeholders must be established.

Advantages	Challenges
• Schools are critical to the success of family-friendly communities and residents in densifying communities are often forced to attend out-of-district schools for many years until population numbers can support the approval and construction of a new neighbourhood school.	• Investment in schools, services, and amenities tends to be attached to the existing community size and demographics. A lack of existing schools, services, and amenities can discourage families from living in a revitalizing or growing community.
• This approach acknowledges that transit oriented developments are ideal locations for family-friendly housing and that public transit plays a key role in housing affordability.	• Investment in transit, schools, and public facilities are often managed by different departments and levels of government, therefore numerous partnerships are often required.

Advantages (cont.)	Challenges (cont.)
• There is significant potential to coordinate transit service, libraries, child care facilities, and school investments with land use to support desired affordable housing goals, while creating a livelier environment and a more efficient use of land. • Transit-oriented development plans can be accompanied by appropriate density and voluntary inclusionary housing policies, thereby supporting municipal family-friendly and affordable housing targets and encouraging future transit ridership.	

Legislative References

Local Government Act, RSBC. 2015, c-1: Part 14: Planning and Land Use Management, Division 4: Official Community Plans

Local Government Act, RSBC. 2015, c-1: Part 14: Planning and Land Use Management, Division 7: Development Permits, Section 488: Designation of Development Permit Areas

7 PARTNERSHIPS AND ALTERNATIVE DELIVERY METHODS

While policy and regulation may help influence the construction of new housing, maintaining affordability often requires additional agreements, partnerships, and collaboration. Many child-friendly amenities, including schools, day cares, and programs, fall under the jurisdiction of other levels of government, therefore, inter-agency partnerships are required to support the creation of complete, livable, and affordable communities for all residents, including families.

Fast-Tracking the Development Approval Process
Municipalities have the ability to prioritize and fast-track developments which meet predetermined policy objectives. Typically associated with the development of affordable housing, fast-tracking child and family-friendly housing developments could significantly contribute to the creation of child and family-friendly communities over time. Fast-tracking development approval processes may help reduce developer costs associated with holding undeveloped land and encourages the timely development of new housing that meets municipal objectives. Fast-tracking family-friendly housing developments could either be accomplished by moving family-friendly housing projects to the highest priority in the application review process and/or assigning an additional staff resource to help developers and investors navigate the review and approval process for these projects. This approach would be most effective if aligned with affordability targets that meet the needs of a broad range of families.

Advantages	Challenges
• Fast-tracking family-friendly housing developments supports timely construction and decreases financing and holding costs for developers. These cost savings may then be transferred to families and residents to increase affordability.	• Ongoing monitoring is required to ensure that fast-tracking approvals does not result in a decrease in the quality of planning and urban design decisions over time.

Advantages (cont.)	Challenges (cont.)
• A more efficient approval process means more efficient use of limited developer and municipal staff time and resources. • Fast-tracking priority developments can help municipalities meet the high need for suitable, family-friendly housing developments in BC communities.	• Fast-tracking may require staff training or the assignment of additional staff, potentially creating additional implementation costs for the municipality. • Some people may complain about preferential treatment unless fast-tracking requirements are clearly laid out in municipal policy.

Legislative References

Local Government Act, RSBC. 2015, c-1: Part 14: Planning and Land Use Management, Division 6: Development Approval Information Requirements, Section 484: Development Approval Information

Local Government Act, RSBC. 2015, c-1: Part 14: Planning and Land Use Management, Division 6: Development Approval Information Requirements, Section 490: General Authority

Housing Agreements

Housing Agreements[8] are a type of legal agreement, supported by bylaw, between a municipality and a developer, landlord, or property owner whereby a predetermined percentage of homes are reserved for long-term affordable rental housing. These contractual agreements may specify the allowable types of tenure, rental rates, sale and share prices, accessibility provisions, and/or ongoing management of the housing units. The strength of housing agreements lies in the fact that they are filed and registered in the Land Titles Office, thus ensuring that the homes remain affordable even if management or ownership changes.

Advantages	Challenges
<ul><li>When in place, these agreements help ensure the long-term affordability of housing units and may be applied to developments on municipally-owned land or through municipal capital grants.</li><li>Housing agreements may allow municipalities to support non-profit housing organizations and incentivize affordable housing development with minimal cost.</li><li>Coupled with density and/or tax incentives, housing agreements may allow municipalities to encourage the development of family-friendly housing in a broad range of communities.</li></ul>	<ul><li>Investors are often concerned that rents under housing agreements will not be allowed to keep pace with market growth or with escalation in operating and maintenance costs.</li><li>When a development project is required to include affordable rental units, developers may prefer to retain ownership of the units rather than turn ownership over to the municipality or a non-profit.</li><li>Developers and non-profit housing providers may be resistant to any agreement registered on title because it limits their ability to adapt to unforeseen market and client changes over time.</li></ul>

Legislative References

Land Title Act, RSBC. 1996, c-250: Part 14: Registration of Title to Charges, Division 3: Certificate of Pending Litigation, Section 219: Registration of Covenant as to Use and Alienation

Local Government Act, RSBC. 2015, c-1: Part 14: Planning and Land Use Management, Division 4: Tax Rates and Exemptions, Section 396: Tax Exemptions Under Partnering Agreement

Local Government Act, RSBC. 2015, c-1: Part 14: Planning and Land Use Management, Division 5: Zoning Bylaws, Section 483: Housing Agreements for Affordable Housing and Special Needs Housing

Community Charter, SBC. 2003, c-26.: Division 7: Permissive Exemptions, Section 226: Revitalization Tax Exemptions

Municipal Children's Advocate

Communities play a crucial role in the social, physical, mental, and economic health of families. Many of the features which most support child and family–friendliness – access to neighbourhood schools, child care, and public facilities – are not solely regulated or funded by local governments and may fall under the jurisdiction of other agencies and levels of governments. Municipalities have the ability to work with all levels of government, community, and business sectors to support healthy child development, care, and learning. In order to support child-friendliness, it is advisable to designate an in-house municipal children's advocate. This advocate can help municipal departments support child and youth consultation, review municipal plans and policies to ensure children's safety and security are considered, ensure funding is allocated toward child-friendly services and amenities, and facilitate partnerships with school boards, public agencies, and other levels of government. A municipal children's advocate serves as a voice for families to ensure that the design and management of housing and services will meet their needs.

Advantages	Challenges
• Reviews and advises Council and staff on the development, implementation and assessment of City policies and services related to children, youth and families. • Supports and facilitates partnerships between municipal governments and school boards for matters relating to new, proposed, and retired school sites.	• Requires additional staff capacity and training. • May require the development of additional municipal policies and procedures to support the work of a children's advocate. • Can be difficult to foster ongoing partnerships and participation with other agencies, departments, and levels of government.

Advantages (cont.)	Challenges (cont.)
• Supports children and youth to have a voice in civic decision-making and addresses barriers to participation and engagement for children, youth, and families. • Initiates and works on projects that enhance access, inclusion and engagement of children, youth and families. • Engages in outreach to disseminate information and encourage participation from constituent communities.	

Legislative References

Local Government Act, RSBC. 2015, c-1: Part 14: Planning and Land Use Management, Division 4: Official Community Plans, Section 475: Consultation During Development of Official Community Plan

Community Charter, SBC. 2003, c-26: Part 5: Municipal Government and Procedures, Division 4 — Committees, Commissions and Other Bodies

Support Capacity within the Non-Profit Housing Sector
Most public sector housing in British Columbia was constructed in the 1970s and 1980s, the result of partnerships and agreements between governments, non-profits, co-operatives, and mission-driven organizations. Government contributions served as the primary source of funding for affordable housing, thereby leaving the sector vulnerable to cutbacks and restrictive operating agreements that limited the flexibility of non-profits to respond to market changes. Since the 1980s, investment in public housing has been largely stalled and existing public sector housing units are approaching the end of their useful lives. Fortunately, funding for social housing is being widely reinstated and local governments now have the opportunity to benefit from accessing capital for non-profit housing initiatives.

To address housing affordability, local governments are again looking to the non-profit housing sector as partners in providing affordable, family-friendly housing. Local governments can support non-profit housing organizations through offering tax and fee exemptions, fast-tracking development application reviews, reducing parking requirements, allowing density and asset transfers between non-profits, and developing community land trusts. Municipalities may also allow developer's contributions of cash, serviced land, or constructed units to non-profit housing organizations in lieu of local amenity contributions. Developing and leveraging partnerships with local and regional housing organizations would enable municipalities to address the needs of a wide demographic of residents – including families – by diversifying the type, tenure, and cost of affordable housing across a broad range of communities and in high-growth areas.

Advantages	Challenges
• Local governments may support non-profit or co-operative housing organizations through fast-tracked development approvals, fee waivers, property tax exemptions, and offering right-of-first-refusal for public lands.	• Property tax exemptions and fee waivers for affordable housing often require the creation and management of housing agreements.

Advantages (cont.)	Challenges (cont.)
• Non-profit housing organizations can facilitate the development of affordable housing units and, through housing agreements, manage and maintain the affordability of these units over time. • Shared-equity ownership, like that offered through organizations like Habitat for Humanity, reinvests gains in the value of an owned home back into affordable housing. This helps eliminate speculation for investment purposes, creating an ideal environment for families who plan on living in the home and building equity over time.	• Shared-equity ownership homes will never be sold on the open market and, therefore, should not be assessed on the open market. Market assessment can create significant issues for non-profits with respect to property transfer and speculation taxes. This issue needs to be revisited at the provincial level. • Non-profits sometimes experience neighbourhood resistance to increased affordable housing density. Ongoing engagement and public education processes may be needed to address this resistance.

Legislative References

Local Government Act, RSBC. 2015, c-1: Part 14: Planning and Land Use Management, Division 4: Tax Rates and Exemptions, Section 396: Tax Exemptions Under Partnering Agreement

Local Government Act, RSBC. 2015, c-1: Part 14: Planning and Land Use Management, Division 5: Zoning Bylaws, Section 483: Housing Agreements for Affordable Housing and Special Needs Housing

Community Charter, SBC. 2003, c-26.: Division 7: Permissive Exemptions, Section 226: Revitalization Tax Exemptions

Community Charter, SBC. 2003, c-26: Part 5: Municipal Government and Procedures, Division 4 — Committees, Commissions and Other Bodies

8 THE TRANSACTIONAL NATURE OF PLANNING POLICY

"Land is a particularly complicated factor in capitalism, as it is both a precondition for all commodities' production and circulation, and a strange sort of commodity in and of itself."
Samuel Stein[9]

The high cost of land across British Columbia has become a dominant social and political issue and is one that disproportionately impacts families. Addressing housing need – including the lack of larger units and other family-friendly housing types – is a complex question that depends on the type and supply of housing that is constructed, the number of vacant properties available, the policies of current and future governments, and the management of land economics at both the site and city scale. There is an overwhelming public belief that, if the supply of housing is increased, then overall housing prices will decrease. While the principles of supply and demand do apply to a certain extent, research has shown that abruptly increasing densification through the relaxation of zoning regulations may have the reverse effect, resulting in higher per-unit costs and increased land values. A solid understanding of land economics can help planners understand and predict the impact and outcome of policy and regulation and can support the successful negotiation of desired land uses, building forms, and public amenities.

The development industry is first and foremost a business, therefore, the successful development of real estate must result in a profitable return. While family-friendly housing may be highly desired by a municipality, most developers will build in order to maximize profit, whether or not the development meets a municipality's long-range objectives. Larger, family-sized units generally take longer to sell and sell for less per square foot than their studio and one bedroom counterparts, making them less attractive to developers and investors for condominiums and purpose-built rentals alike. As a result, many local governments across the province have implemented policies and regulations that incentivize – or outright require - the construction of units with higher bedroom counts in an attempt to create more family-friendly units in their urban centres. However, while policy and regulation may help influence the construction of new, larger units, municipalities are neither able to control who will occupy those units, nor how much they are willing to pay for them. Without additional support from other levels of government, housing providers, and community partners, these units may remain out of reach for many families as they compete for space in the housing market.

Proformas

A proforma is a set of calculations – based on industry trends, standards, and estimations – that anticipates the financial return a proposed real estate development is likely to generate. Proformas allow developers to "test-drive" various development scenarios by using current market rates to estimate the hard and soft costs of development, probable sales or rental revenues, and the net anticipated return on their investment. They allow developers to understand, in quantifiable terms, the maximum value that can be paid for land, the financial costs of planning and rezoning applications, the cash value of amenity and affordable housing contributions, and the optimal distribution of unit types in a proposed development.

Proformas allow developers to calculate the income and non-income generating uses within a project in relation to the hard and soft costs of construction, design, and development. Delays caused by rezoning, public hearings, community resistance, changes in Council, or refusal of the development application can have significant financial implications for developers in terms of additional fees, charges, or carrying costs. Developers are less likely to propose developments on "riskier" parcels of land due to the financial implications of stalled or cancelled projects.

Policy and regulatory requirements for affordable or specialized housing units may present significant financial challenges to developers. For example, a policy which requires the inclusion of affordable units – without the provision of density bonuses or other incentives for developers – means that developers need to achieve these requirements within the normal profit margins of a project. When profit margins are too low, a developer may find it difficult to secure financing for a project and may choose to invest elsewhere. Requiring developers to decrease the selling price of a percentage of units without reductions to the hard or soft costs of construction may create a development proposal that is not viable for private sector builders.

To illustrate the general cost implications of policy and regulatory requirements, let's explore a proforma summary example for a hypothetical apartment development. In this example, 25 market apartments would be constructed, including 6 studio apartments, 9 - 1 bedroom apartments, 5 - 2 bedroom apartments, and 5 - 3 bedroom apartments[i].

Anticipated Project Revenues
    Number of Units   25
    Average Selling Price Per Unit $500,000
    Gross Revenue $12,500,000
    Less Commissions and Fees $750,000

Net Anticipated Revenues   **$11,750,000**

Project Costs
    Land Acquisition $1,200,000
    Transfer Tax $20,000
    Financing Costs on Land Acquisition $75,000

Subtotal - Land and Related Costs   **$1,295,000**

Hard and Soft Construction Costs
    Rezoning, On-Site Servicing and Connections $165,000
    Hard Construction Costs $6,500,000
    Landscaping $90,000
    Soft Costs $575,000
    Contingency on Hard and Soft Costs $350,000
    Financing Fees and Holding Costs $450,000
    Property Taxes $85,000

Subtotal Hard and Soft Construction Costs   **$8,215,000**

Developer's Profit   **$2,240,000**
    Profit Margin on Revenues/Value   18%
    Profit Margin on Costs   22%

---

i These numbers have been rounded for clarity and legibility. To review the full proformas, please see Appendix C.

Using the above proforma template, planners can begin to understand the financial implications of various municipal policies and regulations. For example, if a municipality implements a policy stating that 25% of units in a new development must be affordable, then the same twenty-five unit apartment building would consist of nineteen market units and six affordable units. In the absence of density bonuses, fee waivers, or adjusted parking requirements, the developer proforma would be impacted as follows:

Anticipated Project Revenues

Number of Units	25
Average Selling Price Per Market Unit	$500,000
Average Selling Price Per Affordable Unit	$350,000
Gross Revenue	$11,600,000
Less Commissions and Fees	$700,000
Net Anticipated Revenues	**$10,900,000**

Project Costs

Land Acquisition	$1,200,000
Transfer Tax	$20,000
Financing Costs on Land Acquisition	$75,000
Subtotal - Land and Related Costs	**$1,295,000**

Hard and Soft Construction Costs

Rezoning, On-Site Servicing and Connections	$165,000
Hard Construction Costs	$6,500,000
Landscaping	$90,000
Soft Costs	$575,000
Contingency on Hard and Soft Costs	$350,000
Financing Fees and Holding Costs	$525,000
Property Taxes	$80,000
Subtotal Hard and Soft Construction Costs	**$8,285,000**

Developer's Profit $1,320,000

Profit Margin on Revenues/Value	11%
Profit Margin on Costs	13%

In this example, the developer would earn a nominal profit, though likely not enough to secure financing for the project or otherwise cover the risks associated with developing the site. If incentives were unavailable, the developer would need to increase the average market unit prices by approximately $49,000 each in order to offset the loss in revenue from the affordable units. If the developer feels that this increase would be accepted by the market, then the project may still be considered viable, particularly on a strategically-located or highly-desirable site.

If, however, the municipality were to consider increasing the density of the site in exchange for affordable housing, the developer could better absorb the cost of these units and recover the reduction in profit without such a significant impact on market consumers. For example, the municipality could increase the allowable density from a FAR of 1.5 to a FAR of 1.8, thereby allowing the developer to either construct an additional unit, and/or increase the overall size of the units in the development. In the following example, the developer could construct 3 studio apartments, 7 - 1 bedroom apartments, 8 - 2 bedroom apartments, and 8 - 3 bedroom apartments, for a total of 26 units. This composition would allow a municipality to address both affordability targets and family-friendly housing objectives through a moderate increase in density.

Anticipated Project Revenues
Number of Units	26
Average Selling Price Per Market Unit[ii]	$580,000
Average Selling Price Per Affordable Unit	$405,000
Gross Revenue	$14,000,000
Less Commissions and Fees	$825,000
Net Anticipated Revenues	**$13,175,000**

Project Costs
Land Acquisition	$1,200,000
Transfer Tax	$20,000
Financing Costs on Land Acquisition	$75,000
Subtotal - Land and Related Costs	**$1,295,000**

ii The average selling price per unit has increased because the number of larger units with higher bedroom counts in the building has increased. Similarly, commissions and fees are higher due to the higher average selling cost and increased number of units.

Hard and Soft Construction Costs

Rezoning, On-Site Servicing and Connections	$165,000
Hard Construction Costs	$7,500,000
Landscaping	$90,000
Soft Costs	$700,000
Contingency on Hard and Soft Costs	$400,000
Financing Fees and Holding Costs	$580,000
Property Taxes	$95,000
Subtotal Hard and Soft Construction Costs	**$9,530,000**
Developer's Profit	**$2,350,000**
Profit Margin on Revenues/Value	17%
Profit Margin on Costs	20%

This increase in density would allow the developer to recover the cost of the affordable housing units, while encouraging the development of larger, family-friendly units. Compared to the original baseline scenario, the developer would be able to provide eight two-bedroom and eight three bedroom units - for an overall increase of six larger units - while maintaining the municipality's target of 25% affordable units. In this situation, a modest increase in density would allow both the developer and municipality to benefit from the construction of the proposed project.

As the above examples illustrate, it is critical that planners maintain a solid understanding and awareness of local hard and soft construction costs, land values, typical housing costs, rent levels, and vacancy rates in order to understand – and negotiate – how changes to one aspect of a municipal housing policy or zoning bylaw may impact a project in terms of unit type, affordability, distribution, and overall feasibility. With this understanding, municipalities can begin to align their objectives with private development activities, thereby supporting mutually-beneficial development outcomes.

ENDNOTES

1. Register, Richard. Ecocities: Rebuilding Cities in Balance with Nature, Revised ed. Gabriola Island: New Society Publishers, 2006, p. 6.

2. Business Dictionary. "Policies and Procedures." 2017. Accessed May 18, 2017. http://www.businessdictionary.com/definition/policies-and-procedures.html

3. City of Belfast. A Plan Fit for Children: Health at the Heart of the Local Development Plan, June 2017. https://www.belfasthealthycities.com/sites/default/files/publications/A%20Plan%20Fit%20for%20Children.pdf (accessed September 1, 2019).

4. Metro Vancouver Regional Housing. 2012 What Works: Affordable Housing Initiatives in Metro Vancouver Municipalities. Report. November 2012. http://www.metrovancouver.org/services/regional-planning/PlanningPublications/1267_WhatWorks_LR.pdf (accessed August 3, 2019), pp. 8-11.

5. Beaumont zoning bylaw

6. Province of British Columbia. Residential Rental Tenure Zoning – Bulletin https://www2.gov.bc.ca/assets/gov/british-columbians-our-governments/local-governments/planning-land-use/residential_rental_zoning_bulletin1.pdf Ministry of Municipal Affairs and Housing, July 3, 2018. (accessed July 2, 2019).

7. Beasley, Larry. Vancouverism. Vancouver: UBC Press, 2019, p 331.

8. Province of British Columbia. Land Use Agreements Between Local Governments & Landowners. https://www.placetocallhome.ca/-/media/sf/project/placetocallhome/pdfs/canada-national-housing-strategy.pdf (accessed September 6, 2019).

9. Stein, Samuel. Capital City: Gentrification and the Real Estate State. London: Verso, 2019, p. 35.

PART III: DESIGN GUIDELINES

"Play is often talked about as if it were a relief from seriours learning. But, for children, play is serious learning. Play is really the work of childhood."
Fred Rogers

If the basis of learning is experience, then, arguably, children need full access to a wide range of urban spaces and experiences in order to develop into well-rounded members of society. Cross-disciplinary research by psychologists, sociologists, and designers has shown that limited access to community life contributes to a loss of motivation, confidence, and – ultimately – independence as children enter into adulthood[1]. Children explore their environment within a context of limited life experience, scarce financial resources, and minimal independent mobility and are vulnerable due to their age, size, experience, and status in society. As a result, children's experience in a community closely mirrors the experiences of other vulnerable populations – women, seniors, persons living with disabilities, and low income residents. Addressing children's ability to engage in their communities, to move around their cities, and to access clean, open green spaces may, in fact, help all residents lead happier, healthier, and more fulfilling lives.

At the city scale, child-friendly planning generally takes three forms: the colocation of housing with family-friendly land uses; the ability to safely move around the city by foot, bicycle, and public transportation; and the provision of schools, public spaces, and services that support urban family life. Busy, unplayable streets are increasingly being reimagined as public spaces, providing common ground for play, movement, socialization, and community life. A city that considers vulnerability in its design has within it an inherent flexibility and margin for error; it does not protect children from their mistakes, but rather allows children to learn from them. Child-friendly cities do not aim to provide more segregated places for children, but more integrated places for people.

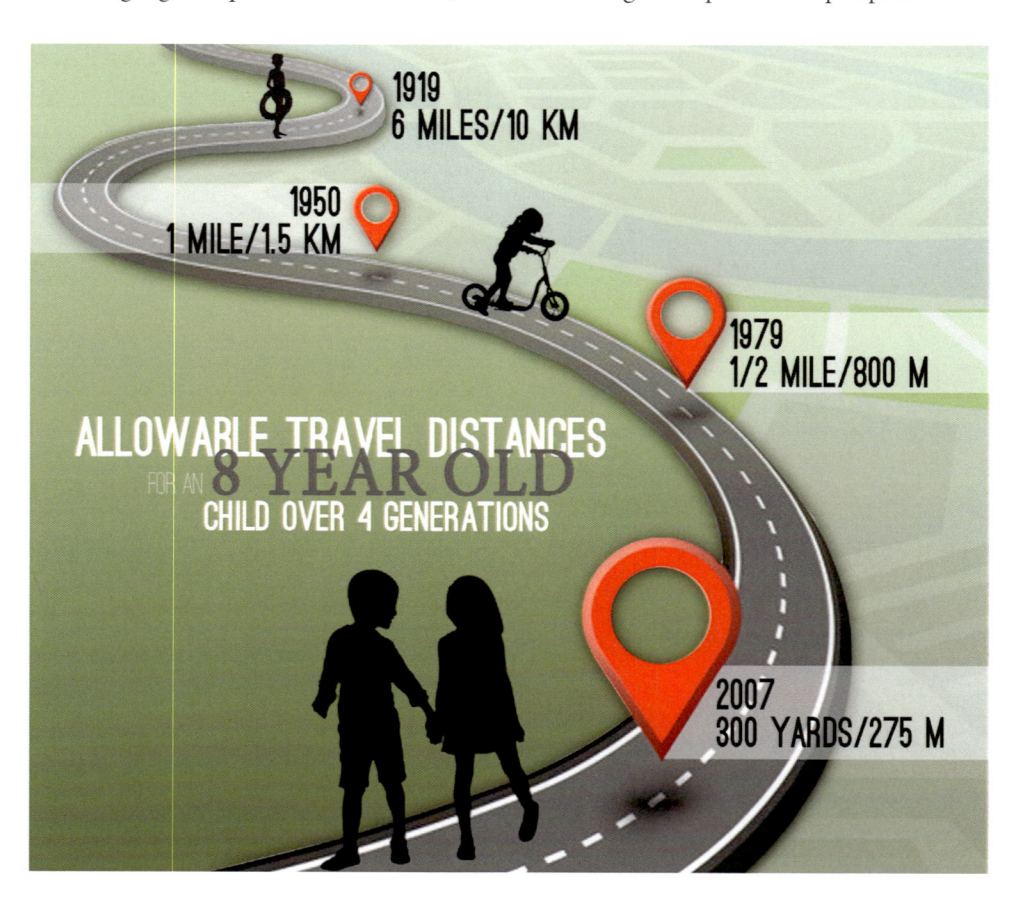

FIG. 8.1
ALLOWABLE TRAVEL DISTANCES AT AGE EIGHT

ALLOWABLE TRAVEL DISTANCES FOR AN 8 YEAR OLD CHILD OVER 4 GENERATIONS

1919 — 6 MILES/10 KM
1950 — 1 MILE/1.5 KM
1979 — 1/2 MILE/800 M
2007 — 300 YARDS/275 M

Yet, the decision to meet the needs of children and their families need not only be a theoretical one. While children may have limited spending power, their parents and caregivers do not. To build and maintain an effective, animated, and successful community, planners and designers must address the needs of families as an important source of daytime activity, revenue, vibrancy, and participation. New and infill development has the potential to provide housing for people, influence well-being, stimulate the economy, enhance social cohesion, and protect the environment.

The design of the built environment shapes the way social and spatial systems function and the users, residents, and visitors they support or attract. Urban environments, in turn, influence how society nurtures and cares for its children, children's ability to develop resilience and independence, and the future physical and emotional health of our society as a whole. However, the needs of children – like the needs of adults – are not homogenous and differ based on age, ability, and personality. Key to planning child-friendly cities is an understanding of children's evolving developmental, social, and spatial needs[2]. A well-designed built environment is integral to creating healthy, inclusive, and resilient communities that support choice and independence throughout a resident's lifetime.

9   DEVELOPMENTAL STAGES

Children are hard wired to learn through experience. As children grow and mature, so too should their ability to independently navigate the world. In order to develop to their full potential, children require frequent, responsive, and interesting interactions with both adults and children within a safe, stimulating physical environment. Poor planning and design, including crowded or inadequate housing, limited access to nature, unsafe streets, poor public spaces, and a lack of local child-centered services, make it more difficult for children to explore and learn from their environment. In short, the way that urban environments are planned, designed, maintained, and managed has a direct impact on the lived experiences, social interactions, and developmental outcomes of children.

A child's spatial needs evolve parallel to their social and physical experiences. From being carried in a caregiver's arms to exploring a local playground, children's confidence, independence, and worldview are closely tied to their experiences in their home community. To create environments that meet children's broad physical, social, cognitive, emotional, and spatial needs, it is necessary to take a closer look at the stages of a child's physical and psychological development – and their related social and spatial needs – as they evolve over time.

Early Childhood (0-4 years)
In early childhood, a child's world consists primarily within an arm's length of their caregivers. Babies and toddlers are almost entirely dependent on their caregivers and their early spatial experiences are generally limited to the home, specialized play and care facilities, healthcare facilities, and the places their caregivers visit with them. The design of homes and local community networks, therefore, may have the ability to exert the greatest influence on the social and emotional health of children in this age group.

As children progress through early childhood, their need for exploration and experimentation increases beyond the immediate reach of their caregiver, setting the foundation for later independence, resilience, and self-sufficiency. The spatial needs of young children differ from those of school-age children, adolescents, and young adults. During early childhood, children:

- Experience the world at the scale of the room;
- Have a limited independent range of mobility and are always found with caregivers as they travel around the neighbourhood and city;
- Explore the environment using their body, including tasting, touching, moving, manipulating, seeing, and hearing;
- Begin to become interested in spatial details and, by age three, may use prominent landmarks to describe the locations of places;
- Cannot cross streets independently, even with crosswalks and lights;
- Have an average walking speed of between 0.52 m/s (age 0-2) and 0.84 m/s (age 3-6)[3], roughly equivalent to that of a senior using a walker;
- Are particularly vulnerable to air pollution and environmental toxins and may be sensitive to noise;
- Tend to play alongside, rather than with, peers; and
- Begin to show preference for friends of the same gender. At the age of three, girls tend to prefer small group activities with other girls while, by age four, boys tend to prefer large group interactions with other boys[4].

Can You Make the Light?

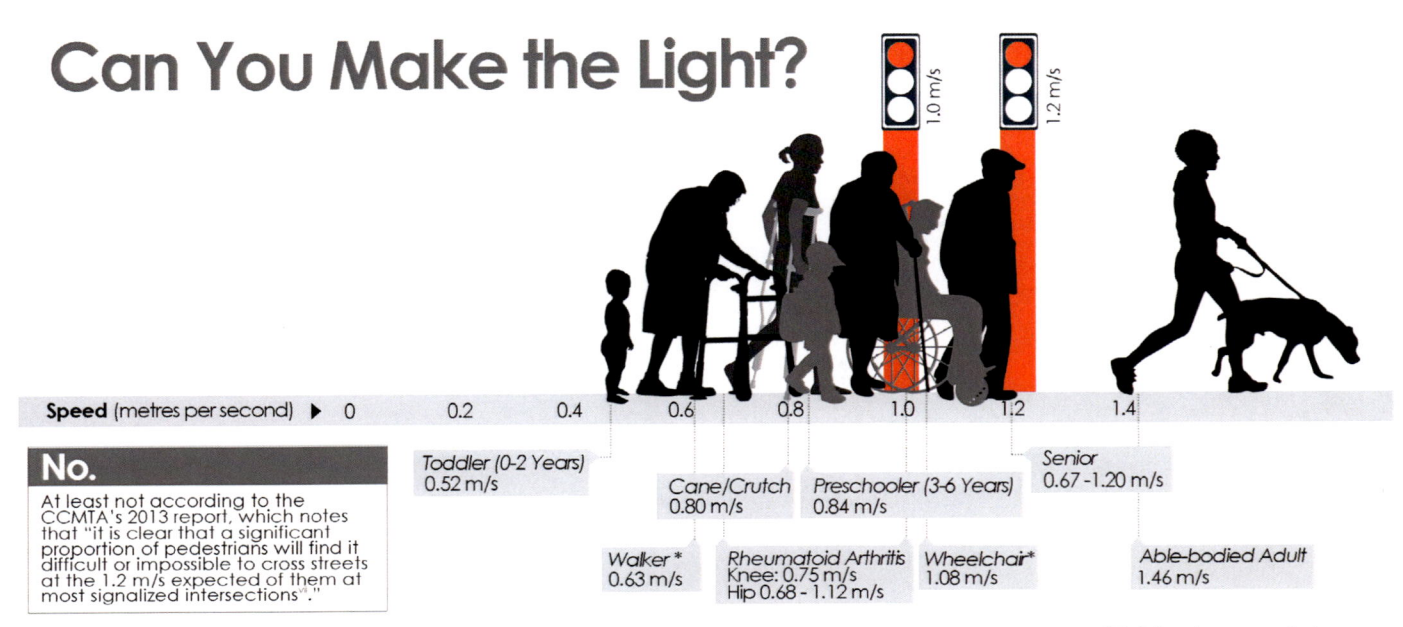

Speed (metres per second) ▶ 0   0.2   0.4   0.6   0.8   1.0   1.2   1.4

- Toddler (0-2 Years) 0.52 m/s
- Walker* 0.63 m/s
- Cane/Crutch 0.80 m/s
- Rheumatoid Arthritis Knee: 0.75 m/s Hip 0.68 - 1.12 m/s
- Preschooler (3-6 Years) 0.84 m/s
- Wheelchair* 1.08 m/s
- Senior 0.67 - 1.20 m/s
- Able-bodied Adult 1.46 m/s

Traffic signals: 1.0 m/s, 1.2 m/s

No. At least not according to the CCMTA's 2013 report, which notes that "it is clear that a significant proportion of pedestrians will find it difficult or impossible to cross streets at the 1.2 m/s expected of them at most signalized intersections⁽⁾."

* Limitation of user unspecified

School-Age Children (5-12)

By school-age, a child's environment has typically expanded from the confines of their home to include a variety of neighbourhood, educational, and community spaces. School-age children are increasingly able to explore public spaces, at first within eyesight of their caregivers and, later, independently or with friends. School-age children generally explore their environments within semi-defined visual boundaries; they can travel independently to a pre-determined street corner, hedgerow, or public park, exploring and challenging their own physical limitations through active play. Children of this age begin to develop a mental map of their communities - based primarily on landmarks, paths, and nodes - and are able to describe the spatial relationships between their home, school, friends' houses, and other frequently-visited places within the community.

School-age children develop self-regulation skills though exploring the social and physical limitations of their environments. Research has demonstrated that children who have access to private space within their home have greater task persistence and fewer behavioural problems than children living in crowded homes[5]. Furthermore, children with stable home environments are more likely to complete high school, score higher on academic achievement tests, and are less likely to become pregnant as teenagers, regardless of neighbourhood characteristics, parental education, or family structure[6]. School-age children[7]:

- Experience the world at the neighbourhood scale;
- Have rapidly developing navigational skills and understand the spatial relationships between their homes, schools, parks, and other frequently-visited places;
- Experience an increasingly independent range of mobility and may be permitted to travel unaccompanied throughout their immediate neighbourhood, generally within predetermined boundaries;
- Can cross streets independently using crosswalks and crossing lights;
- Have limited spending money and may have access to a mobile phone;
- Girls tend to engage in social, imaginative, and cooperative play and often become more discerning about the condition and variety of play equipment. Girls may begin to gravitate to the outer perimeter of playgrounds in small social groups[8];
- Boys often begin to engage in more active play - on or around, rather than with, equipment - in the centre of playgrounds and may use up to ten times more space for play than girls[9];
- Mixed-sex play groups tend to include larger groups of children and may be focused around a large group game or dramatic and fantasy play; and
- Children of all genders practice physical skills such as jumping rope or riding a bike in order to get better.

Adolescents (10-19)
Constituting just over 10% of the population of British Columbia, adolescents are legally considered to be children up to the age of 19. Adolescents are generally able to travel freely around their community and beyond, by foot, bicycle, or transit alone or with peers and may, themselves, be primary or secondary caregivers of infants and school-age children. Adolescents often engage in casual group socialization activities with their peers, which may be misinterpreted as loitering or trouble making and may result in discrimination. Design for this age group is typically focused on the creation of skate parks and often overlooks the need for

passive social gathering spaces where adolescents may spend long periods of time without arousing suspicion or needing to purchase goods or services.

The built environment influences health and well-being through opportunities to be physically active, play, socialize, and access services. Healthy environments - with ample opportunities for physical activity and social engagement - have been proven to have positive impacts on graduation rates and educational outcomes, positively influence adult lifestyles and activity levels, reduce delinquency, and support successful employment for young adults. As independence and autonomy increase with age, it is easy to assume that the needs of older children and young adults are adequately met by policies and programs intended for adults. In reality, however, many adolescents "age-out" of child care, recreational activities, and other services, leaving them ineligible for programs intended for children, but unsupported by programs intended for adults. Adolescents:

- Experience the world at the neighbourhood or city scale;
- Have well-developed navigational skills and can navigate to both new and frequently-visited places with the help of maps, directions, or signage;
- Experience an increasingly independent range of mobility and may be able to travel independently to a number of destinations within the city;
- May be employed in the community and may have access to spending money;
- May or may not have the ability or desire to drive;
- Likely have access to a mobile phone;
- May face discrimination due to misconceptions and generalizations about their age and activities;
- May show interest in civic processes, activism, and advocacy, and may express concern regarding a number of social, economic, and environmental issues;
- Enjoy hanging out and socializing with friends; and
- Often lack spaces to gather and socialize that do not require payment or place time limitations on use.

Young Adults (15-24)

Young adults include all persons between the ages of fifteen and twenty-four years. Young adults generally have full, independent access to the city and all public spaces and facilities. Young adults may be engaged in civic processes and political discussions and may be disproportionately impacted by rising rent and housing prices, inconsistent access to transit, and opportunities for local employment. Young adults are capable of traveling independently around the city by foot, bicycle, transit, or private vehicle - alone or with peers - and may, themselves, be primary or secondary caregivers of infants and school-age children. Young adults:

- Experience the world at the city or global scale;
- Have well-developed navigational skills and can navigate to both new and frequently-visited places with the help of maps, directions, or signage;
- Experience an independent range of mobility and are able to travel independently to most destinations within the city;
- May be employed in the community and likely have access to spending money;
- May live independently from parents with or without roommates or partners;
- May or may not have the ability or desire to drive;
- Likely have access to a mobile phone;
- May face discrimination due to misconceptions and generalizations about their age and activities;
- May be involved in civic processes, activism, and advocacy, and may express concern regarding a number of social, economic, and environmental issues;
- May be disproportionately impacted by high costs of living, inadequate public transportation networks, or a lack of local employment opportunities; and
- May themselves be caregivers or parents to young children.

10 DESIGN GUIDELINES

The guidelines that are proposed herein attempt to address the spatial needs of children and their families at the building, block, and city scale. The intent of these guidelines is not to describe purpose-built, segregated spaces for children, but rather to support the co-creation of a multi-generational city where children are considered as valuable and equal members of society.

Centered around nine key principles, the guidelines are intended to help municipalities, planners, designers, politicians, developers, and residents co-create communities that are responsive, liveable, and equitable for families of all sizes and compositions. The design principles that are explored within this section are:

Principle 1: Housing Diversity
Child-friendly communities respond to the existing and anticipated social context by providing a mix of housing types, tenures, and sizes for residents of a variety of ages, incomes, and household compositions. Homes should be designed to be flexible and adaptable to residents' changing needs over time.

Principle 2: Built Form and Unit Design
Good family-friendly design delineates the public realm from private spaces, allowing space for children to play, while contributing to the character of the streetscape and community. Individual dwellings should have sufficient area to ensure functional, well-organized, and comfortable spaces for residents.

Principle 3: Sustainability
Buildings and homes should incorporate passive environmental design features - including passive solar heating and natural ventilation – to reduce maintenance and operating costs, while contributing to overall community sustainability. Sustainability targets should be included as explicit policy objectives with respect to development at the building, neighbourhood, and city scale.

Principle 4: Private Amenities
Access to private and semi-private open space provides space for children to play outdoors and helps offset the loss of private garage and yard space for families living in smaller, denser developments. Access to private and shared amenity space supports the opportunity for pet ownership.

Principle 5: Local Character and Context
The architectural form, articulation and scale of a development should relate to and enhance the local character and context of the area. Family-friendly buildings consider opportunities for passive supervision and acknowledge the role of neighbours in keeping children safe.

Principle 6: Landscape
Landscape design provides opportunities for residents' interaction with nature and supports the healthy growth of local plant and tree species. A child-friendly landscape provides recreation and amenity space, opportunities for social interaction, and connection with the natural environment.

Principle 7: Full Spectrum CPTED
Good design supports a wide variety of public and private spaces and optimizes safety and security within the development and the public domain through appropriate landscaping and sensitive building and community design. Full Spectrum CPTED enables passive surveillance and casual supervision by parents and neighbours to support children's safety.

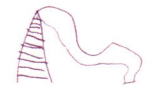

Principle 8: Public Amenities
Residents, including families with children, should have reasonable and safe access to local community services and recreational amenities. A high level of amenity for local residents is the direct result of supporting residential density that is appropriate to the site and context.

Principle 9: Transportation Networks
Safe walking and cycling routes support active living, connect child-specific destinations, and help mitigate real and/or perceived risk associated with independent mobility.

DESIGN GUIDELINES | 71

Design Principles / Design Objectives		Building				Block			City
		1. Housing Diversity	2. Built Form and Unit Design	3. Sustainability	4. Private Amenities	5. Local Character and Context	6. Landscape	7. Full Spectrum CPTED	8. Public Amenities	9. Transportation Networks
1.1	Missing Middle	●	●	●	●	●	●	●	●	
1.2	Family Units	●	●		●	●		●	●	●
1.3	On-site Child Care	●	●		●	●		●	●	●
1.4	Universal Design	●	●		●		●	●	●	●
2.1	Public Domain Interface	●	●		●	●	●	●	●	
2.2	Individualization of Homes	●	●		●	●	●	●	●	
2.3	Flexible Layout	●	●		●					
2.4	Adequate Dwelling Size	●	●		●					
2.5	Number of Rooms	●	●		●					
2.6	Storage		●		●			●		
2.7	Bicycle Parking		●	●	●	●		●	●	●
2.8	Sound Attenuation	●	●							
2.9	Privacy and Passive Surveillance		●			●	●	●		
3.1	Solar Access		●	●	●		●	●		
3.2	Natural Ventilation		●	●						
3.3	Passive Environmental Design		●	●			●			
4.1	Private Open Spaces	●	●	●	●	●	●	●		
4.2	Communal Spaces	●	●		●	●	●	●	●	
4.3	Outdoor Play Areas				●	●	●	●	●	

Design Principles / Design Objectives		1. Housing Diversity	2. Built Form and Unit Design	3. Sustainability	4. Private Amenities	5. Local Character and Context	6. Landscape	7. Full Spectrum CPTED	8. Public Amenities	9. Transportation Networks
5.1	Architectural Form	•	•	•	•	•		•	•	
5.2	Building Orientation	•	•	•	•	•		•		
5.3	Adjacent Land Uses	•	•	•	•	•	•	•	•	•
6.1	Landscape Design			•	•	•	•	•	•	•
6.2	Communal Outdoor Spaces	•	•			•	•	•	•	
7.1	Passive Surveillance	•	•			•		•	•	•
7.2	Access	•	•		•			•	•	•
8.1	Local Amenities	•			•		•	•	•	•
8.2	Local Schools	•				•	•	•	•	•
8.3	Parks and Playgrounds		•	•		•	•	•	•	•
8.4	Active and Playful Public Realm		•	•		•	•	•	•	•
9.1	Safe Walking Routes		•	•		•	•	•	•	•
9.2	Vehicle Access		•			•			•	•
9.3	Internal Streets and Laneways		•			•	•	•		•
9.4	Busy Streets					•	•	•	•	•
9.5	Multimodal Pathways			•		•	•	•	•	•

Scales: Building (columns 1–4), Block (columns 5–7), City (columns 8–9).

Design Principles: key goals of a design.
Objectives: set out what the design principles should achieve.
Design Criteria: features and standards that can be used to meet the objectives.

All scales, principles, criteria, and objectives are interrelated.

BUILDING DESIGN

Principle 1: Housing Diversity

Child-friendly communities respond to the existing and anticipated social context by providing a mix of housing types, tenures, and sizes for residents of a variety of ages, incomes, and household compositions. Homes should be designed to be flexible and adaptable to residents' changing needs over time.

Objective 1.1: Missing Middle

Provide a wide variety of "missing middle" housing forms within a community.

Design Criteria

1 Include building and façade details that provide a human scale and where children can relate their height to the scale of development around them.

2 Incorporate missing middle developments – including townhouses, row houses, walk-up apartments, and courtyard housing – across every community as infill development.

3 Developments should consider the spaces between buildings as opportunities for children to gather and play.

4 Family-friendly housing should have reasonable access to schools, transit, parks, retail, and employment opportunities.

5 Provide a variety of tenure options within every community or development, including both market and affordable rental housing options.

Objective 1.2: Family Units

Consider the number, location, and orientation of family-friendly units to support social interaction and cohesion.

Design Criteria

1. Design developments to include twenty to thirty homes per building, up to a maximum of 75 children/ha or 70 children in one project[11].

2. A maximum of 12 units should be serviced by one corridor or entry to support social interaction and neighbourly relationships.

3. Larger developments may include podium courtyards with row houses to support a community scale.

4. Where family units are constructed, family amenities – including on-side child care, playgrounds, courtyards, and shared amenity spaces - should also be incorporated.

DESIGN GUIDELINES | 75

Objective 1.3: On-Site Child Care

Accommodate on-site family child care and recreation options to support residents and local families.

Design Criteria

1. On-site family child care units should be provided at ground level with access to a secure outdoor courtyard, balcony or patio area.

2. Amenity and commercial spaces in family-friendly developments should consider the physical requirements for daycares as it can be difficult to retrofit restaurant or retail spaces at a later date.

3. Developments should consider the incorporation of shared recreation spaces or entertainment rooms that can meet the needs of children, adolescents, and multi-generational families.

Objective 1.4: Universal Design

Universal design features are included within a variety of unit sizes and types to promote flexible housing for all community members.

Design Criteria

1. In townhouses, row houses, and multi-family developments, at least one ground floor dwelling unit should include adaptable design features.

2. A portion of all new three bedroom units should include adaptable design features.

3. Universal design features should be included at the unit, building, and neighbourhood scale that support simple, equitable, and intuitive access[12].

Principle 2: Built Form and Unit Design

Good family-friendly design delineates the public realm from private spaces, allowing space for children to play, while contributing to the character of the streetscape and community. Individual dwellings should have sufficient area to ensure functional, well-organized, and comfortable spaces for residents.

Objective 2.1: Public Domain Interface

Homes are orientated to the street or to a shared courtyard and provide opportunities for passive supervision, social interaction, and physical and visual connectivity.

Design Criteria

1. Each dwelling has direct frontage onto a street or into a shared courtyard.

2. Where included, setbacks are designed to provide amenity space and reduce overshadowing and privacy concerns to neighbouring lots.

3. Dwellings should be designed to layer exterior spaces from the public sidewalk to private porches and balconies that allow children and their families access to semi-private outdoor space.

4. Opportunities should be provided for casual interaction between residents and the public, including the addition of front porches, semi-private courtyards, and seating areas at building entries.

Objective 2.2: Individualization of Homes

Homes are individualized and distinguishable from others on the same street or in the same development.

Design Criteria

1. Individual, ground-oriented homes are identifiable from the public street with the front door and the address visible from the public street or sidewalk.

2. Homes in multi-family developments may be identifiable from the public street via balcony decoration or details, façade treatments, or door and window styles.

3. Entries to each home from internal corridors may be individualized through different door and hardware styles, unique windows and sidelights, variations in corridor width, and façade articulations.

Objective 2.3: Flexible Layout

Unit design and layout is flexible, responsive, and inclusive for residents of different ages, abilities, and lifestyles. Unit design should accommodate live/work arrangements and support the ability to age in place.

Design Criteria

1. All units should be designed, at a minimum, to a visitable standard to support multi-generational use and aging in place.

2. To cater to a wide variety of user and family needs, the design of homes may include:
   - A level, no-step entry into the home;
   - Rooms designed for multiple functions for 24 hour use;
   - At least one washroom on the entry-level floor of the home; and
   - The ability to adapt a ground floor room into a bedroom, work, or study space or the inclusion of more than one master bedroom to accommodate multi-generational families.

3. Residential buildings should target a minimum of 25% family units containing two or more bedrooms in all new market housing and 50% family units in all new non-market housing[13].

4. A minimum of 10% of all units should contain 3 or more bedrooms.

5. Units should incorporate universal design features that would be difficult and costly to retrofit at a later date.

6. Family units should be grouped together on lower floors, near communal areas, or overlooking outdoor play spaces.

Objective 2.4: Adequate Dwelling Size

The home is designed to ensure functional, well-organized, and comfortable spaces for residents.

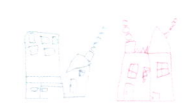

Design Criteria

1. Homes should be designed so that the shared living room is the largest space within the dwelling unit.

2. Living rooms and/or play areas are situated with sightlines to the kitchen to allow for supervision and connectivity within the home.

3. Homes should be designed to incorporate an uninterrupted, circular path of travel connecting the kitchen to the living room so that kids can run around as if running a track.

4. Living rooms have access to a window and receive direct or indirect sunlight for a minimum of 2 hours per day during the winter solstice.

5. Where possible, units should be designed to allow for layout changes over time. For example, walls may be constructed through moveable partitions rather than through drywall construction.

DESIGN GUIDELINES | 79

Objective 2.5: Number of Rooms

Room sizes are appropriate for the intended purpose and number of occupants.

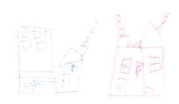

Design Criteria

1 Recommended minimum dwelling unit sizes in row houses and townhouses, excluding storage are[14]:

- 2 bed: 90 m² (970 sqft)
- 3 bed: 112 m² (1200 sqft)
- 4 bed: 125 m² (1350 sqft)

2 Recommended minimum dwelling unit sizes in apartments excluding storage are[15]:

- 1 bed: 46 m² (500 sqft)
- 2 bed: 66 m² (700 sqft)
- 3 bed: 84 m² (900 sqft)
- 4 bed: 105-117 m² (1125 - 1250 sqft)
- 2 bed with in-home family daycare unit: 107-112 m² (1150 - 1200 sqft)
- 3 bed with in-home family daycare unit: 130-139 m² (1400 - 1500 sqft)

3 Dens are designed with sufficient area to support future use as an additional, "inboard" bedroom.

4 The minimum area of any room is 10 m² (approximately 100 sqft) to accommodate a single bed, dresser, desk, and usable floor space for playing or working.

5 At least one bedroom has a minimum area of 12 m² (approximately 120 sqft). Bedrooms have a minimum length and width of 3 m (approximately 10 ft), excluding space for a closet.

6 Kitchens and bathrooms are constructed with adequate space for more than one person and consideration of future accessibility needs (1,500 mm turn radius).

7 Provide a minimum entrance area of 4 m², with a minimum width of 1.5 m. Entrance areas should be able to accommodate four people or a stroller with space for maneuvering.

Objective 2.7: Bicycle Parking

Secure, covered parking facilities are provided for bicycles.

Design Criteria

1 Sufficient space is provided in garages for the secure storage of at least 3 bicycles per household.

2 Bicycle parking includes secure storage for cargo bikes.

3 Multi-family developments may provide space for bicycle share opportunities, including cargo bicycles.

Objective 2.6: Storage

Adequate, well-designed storage is provided in each dwelling.

Design Criteria

1 In addition to storage in kitchens, bathrooms, linen closets, and clothes closets, residents should be provided with minimum storage areas of 5.7 m³.

2 At least 50% of the required storage should be located inside the dwelling unit.

3 The layout of a dwelling should consider a range of storage spaces, including at least one larger space within the unit for storing bulky items such as strollers, suitcases, holiday decorations, or sports equipment. One larger, deep closet near the front entrance is preferred.

DESIGN GUIDELINES | 81

Objective 2.8: Sound Attenuation

Ensure outside noise levels are controlled to acceptable levels in living rooms and bedrooms.

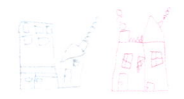

Design Criteria

1. Noise transfer is minimized through the building siting and layout, with window and door openings orientated away from anticipated sources of noise.

2. Building design should group rooms with similar noise requirements together. Noisy areas, including building entries, gathering, and circulation spaces, should be located next to or above each other and quiet spaces, such as bedrooms, should be located next to or above other quiet spaces.

3. Common walls and floors between units and around public areas should be insulated to provide the ability to muffle sound of up to 55 decibels.

4. Sound-insulated wall and flooring materials should be installed between active spaces, such as kitchens or living rooms.

5. Closets may be positioned for use as sound buffers between bedrooms and shared living spaces within units.

6. Shrubs, trees, and vegetation should be incorporated into site landscaping to help buffer noise in combination with other sound attenuating features.

Objective 2.9: Privacy and Passive Surveillance

A balance of interior privacy and exterior surveillance is supported and maintained through building and unit design.

Design Criteria

1. Interior doorways should be staggered so that neighbours are not looking directly into homes.

2. Balconies and private outdoor space should be located in front of living rooms to increase internal privacy, while allowing for passive surveillance of common spaces and the public realm.

DESIGN GUIDELINES | 83

Principle 3: Sustainability

Buildings and homes should incorporate passive environmental design features - including passive solar heating and natural ventilation – to reduce maintenance and operating costs, while contributing to overall community sustainability. Sustainability targets should be included as explicit policy objectives with respect to development at the building, neighbourhood, and city scale.

Objective 3.1: Solar Access

The design of homes optimizes sunlight access to habitable rooms to support passive solar heating in winter and promote a healthy indoor environment.

Design Criteria

1 Living rooms should receive a minimum of 2 hours direct or indirect sunlight between 9 am and 3 pm on the winter solstice (December 21).

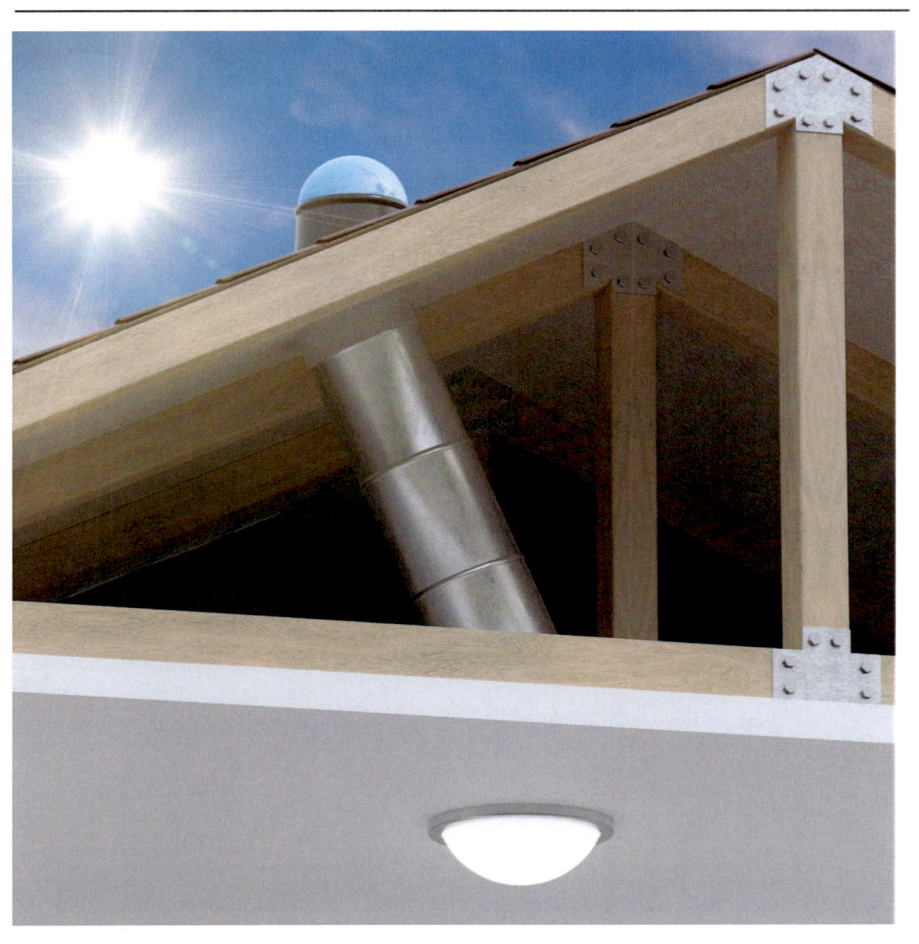

2 Private outdoor spaces should receive a minimum of 2 hours direct sunlight between 9 am and 3 pm on the winter solstice (December 21).

3 All habitable rooms should ensure that a window is visible from 75% of the floor area of a habitable room.

4 Solar tubes may be installed to provide natural light to interior rooms with minimal heat loss.

5 Building heights and setbacks should work together to allow for good daylight access to shared and private open spaces and private homes.

6 Deciduous trees should be incorporated into landscaping to provide shade in the summer and allow for sunlight penetration in the winter.

Objective 3.3: Passive Environmental Design

Buildings and homes incorporate passive environmental design features.

Design Criteria

1 An outdoor area for clothes drying is provided for each dwelling unit.

2 Clothes drying areas of at least 16 linear metres per dwelling are provided and are screened from public view and communal areas.

Objective 3.2: Natural Ventilation

All habitable rooms have access to natural ventilation.

Design Criteria

1 All habitable rooms, with the possible exception of the kitchen and bathroom, should have operable windows and access to natural ventilation.

2 No part of a habitable room should be more than 8 m from a window.

3 Windows are visible and operable from a seated position.

4 Windows on upper floors of buildings do not excessively swing or tilt outwards to prevent children from falling.

… DESIGN GUIDELINES | 85

Principle 4: Private Amenities

Access to private and semi-private open space provides space for children to play outdoors and helps offset the loss of private garage and yard space for families living in smaller, denser developments. Access to private and shared amenity space supports the opportunity for pet ownership.

Objective 4.1: Private Open Spaces

Dwellings provide individual access to private open space and balconies for children to play outdoors.

Design Criteria

1 Private open space is located adjacent to the living room, dining room, or kitchen to extend the living space and support internal privacy.

2 The size of private open space should be proportional to the size of the dwelling and, at a minimum, should allow all members of the household to sit comfortably around a table:

- 1 bed or studio: minimum 85 sqft (approximately 8 sqm)
- 2 bed: minimum 130 sqft (approximately 12 sqm)
- 3+ bedroom: minimum 175 sqft (approximately 16 sqm)

3 Any private balcony or outdoor space will have a minimum usable size[16] of 1.8 m by 2.7 m.

4 At least 25% of the private open space should be covered to provide shade and weather protection.

Objective 4.2: Communal Spaces

Communal areas enhance residential amenity, support safety and connectivity, and promote social interaction between residents.

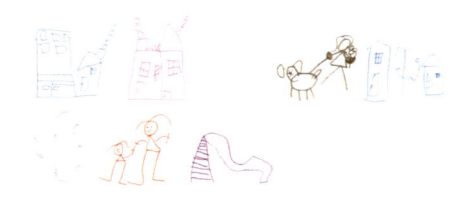

Design Criteria

① Communal open spaces should provide direct, clear access to dwellings and a clear line of sight from habitable rooms to support passive supervision, while maintaining visual privacy.

② Facilities should be provided within communal spaces for a range of age groups and may include:

- Barbeque areas;
- Entertainment or games rooms;
- On-site libraries or reading rooms;
- Common rooms, communal kitchens, or dining areas for communal use or private rental;
- Play equipment or play areas; and
- Swimming pools, gyms, tennis courts, or recreation rooms.

③ Each development should provide an indoor multipurpose room large enough to accommodate 40% of the anticipated adult population of a building[17].

④ Amenities that encourage physical activity should be provided, including a gym room with punching bags, exercise balls, and mats, stationary bicycle-operated video games, a shared activity room for small children with ride-on toys, an outdoor children's exercise circuit, and/or a highly visible and attractive stairwell.

⑤ Communal space should incorporate opportunities for artwork in the form of sculpture, architecture or landscape features.

Objective 4.3: Outdoor Play Areas

Provide outdoor play areas suitable for children of all ages.

Design Criteria

1 Visible, accessible, and safe play space should be provided for children and should be overlooked by common facilities, laundry rooms, and individual dwelling units[18].

2 Communal courtyards and play areas should receive a minimum of two hours of sunlight between the hours of 9:30 am - 11:30 am and/or 1:30 pm - 4:30 pm on the winter solstice (December 21).

3 Communal courtyards should be designed to:
- Be fully open to the sky; and
- Have a minimum dimension of at least 1/3 the height of the perimeter wall to ensure adequate access to sunlight.

4 Total outdoor play area may be divided between one or more locations and may range in size from 130 sqm to 280 sqm per development, providing approximately 10 sqm of dedicated play space per child[19].

5 Play spaces should include a minimum of 1.0 sqm per bedroom (excluding the master bedroom) of preschool children's play areas, with a minimum area of 50 sqm in a courtyard serving 6-12 households[20].

6 A minimum of 1.5 sqm per bedroom (excluding the master bedroom) of outdoor play space should be allocated for elementary school-aged and older children, with a minimum area of 85 sqm and serving up to 60 households. This area can be reduced if there is a playground, sports field, or community facility within 400 m.

7 Opportunities should be provided for active and quiet play by both groups and individuals. Opportunities for children to interact with natural materials, including sand, water, rocks, and vegetation, should be provided.

8 Where possible, washrooms that are accessible to children from outdoor play areas should be provided, particularly where access to individual units from outside is constrained by locked doors and buzzer systems.

9 Shelter from rain, sun, and wind should be provided in outdoor play areas and there should be seating provided for adults to facilitate supervision and socialization.

10 Amenity areas for adolescents should be given special consideration. Informal spaces where teens can congregate should be provided, and can include comfortable seating areas, ball courts, games rooms, gyms, and skateboarding areas.

BLOCK DESIGN

Principle 5: Local Character and Context

The architectural form, articulation and scale of a development should relate to and enhance the local character and context of the area. Family-friendly buildings consider opportunities for passive supervision and acknowledge the role of neighbours in keeping children safe.

Objective 5.1: Architectural Form

The architectural form, design, and scale of development relates to the local character and context of the area.

Design Criteria

① Variation in materials, colours and key elements, such as doors, windows and balconies, should be used to allow for personalization of homes and allow individual homes to be identifiable from the street.

② Building facades should have an appropriate scale and proportion to the streetscape and to a human scale.

③ Building orientation should consider impacts of the development on shadows, wind, and other local climate conditions at street level.

④ Each dwelling should face a street or landscaped courtyard.

⑤ Buildings that include colour, public art, and unique design features provide public amenity and are often preferred by children.

DESIGN GUIDELINES | 89

4. Opportunities should be provided for casual interaction between residents and the public, including seating at building entries, near mailboxes, and in semi-private courtyards adjacent to streets.

5. Low fences and landscaping may be used to delineate between semi-private open space and the adjacent public realm.

Objective 5.3: Adjacent Land Uses

Residential uses for families with children should consider adjacent land uses.

Design Criteria

1. Direct visibility is provided down driveways and walkways from the public street for safety and connectivity.

2. Windows from habitable rooms overlook the public domain to support passive supervision.

3. The front door and address of each ground-oriented dwelling are directly visible from the public street.

Design Criteria

1. Non-residential uses in mixed-use buildings should be provided with separate, distinct pedestrian and vehicle access.

2. Play areas within a multi-family development should not be easily accessible to strangers.

3. Building design should consider the needs of teenagers and older children, particularly when commercial, café, and recreational amenity spaces are provided as part of the development.

Objective 5.2: Building Orientation

Homes are orientated to the street and provide opportunities for passive supervision, casual social interaction, and visual connectivity.

Principle 6: Landscape

Landscape design provides opportunities for residents' interaction with nature and supports the healthy growth of local plant and tree species. A child-friendly landscape provides recreation and amenity space, opportunities for social interaction, and connection with the natural environment.

Objective 6.1: Landscape Design

Landscape design supports the healthy growth of local plant and tree species.

Design Criteria

1. Landscaping should incorporate vegetation that is hardy and of sufficient size to withstand children's play.

2. Local plant and tree species should be incorporated, ideally requiring little to no additional irrigation.

3. Landscape design should incorporate a variety of spaces and opportunities, including:

   - hard and soft landscaping;
   - rain gardens;
   - shade trees;
   - private and shared garden plots;
   - opportunities for composting; and
   - natural and landscape-based play areas.

4. Incorporation of appropriately-sized street trees to support pedestrian comfort, help slow traffic, and provide visual amenity.

5. An ongoing maintenance plan should be provided as part of the landscape plan.

6. Fencing or landscape screening should be provided to protect children from access to potentially dangerous areas such as gas meters, electrical transformers, roads, and steep slopes.

DESIGN GUIDELINES | 91

Objective 6.2: Communal Outdoor Spaces

Communal areas enhance residential amenity, support safety and connectivity, and promote social interaction between residents.

Design Criteria

1 Semi-private indoor communal areas should be connected to a well-designed, outdoor landscaped area.

2 Communal outdoor spaces should not negatively impact the privacy of dwellings.

3 Communal outdoor spaces must be well lit and should be designed with input from a CPTED professional.

4 Communal outdoor spaces should be shared by no more than 100 households.

5 Common outdoor spaces may be shared between multiple developments, provided equitable access, adequate space, and appropriate management is provided.

6 Existing landscape features and site characteristics, including mature trees and rock outcrops, should be retained and integrated into the character of the development wherever possible.

7 Landscaping should support a comfortable microclimate by incorporating:

- shade trees located on the south and west sides of outdoor gathering and play areas;
- a combination of evergreen and deciduous trees to provide shade in summer and sunlight access in winter; and
- where shade trees are not appropriate, common landscaped areas, playgrounds, picnic areas, and courtyards should incorporate shade structures, canopies, pergolas, and/or awnings.

Principle 7: Full Spectrum CPTED

Good design supports a wide variety of public and private spaces and optimizes safety and security within the development and the public domain through appropriate landscaping and sensitive building and community design. Full Spectrum CPTED enables passive surveillance and casual supervision by parents and neighbours to support children's safety.

Objective 7.1: Passive Surveillance

Design supports passive surveillance and casual supervision from the street to homes and from homes to semi-private and public spaces.

Design Criteria

① Shared, semi-private open spaces such as plazas, common areas, and on-site playgrounds must be clearly designated and situated at locations that are easily observable from both dwelling units and common areas.

② Landscaping should not obstruct visibility and may include low groundcover, high-canopy trees, and shrubs up to a maximum of 0.6 m in height around children's play areas, parking areas, and along pedestrian pathways.

③ Landscaping which obstructs natural surveillance and allows intruders to hide should be avoided.

④ Adequate lighting in all semi-private and common areas should be provided.

Objective 7.2: Access

A balance of interior privacy and exterior surveillance is supported and maintained through building and unit design.

Design Criteria

1. Address building features that limit access to and from communal spaces by small children, including locked doors requiring keys or buzzer systems. Elevators and locking fire doors on stairs also may act as obstacles and pose a safety hazard for children.

2. Ensure multiple points of entry to and egress from shared spaces.

CITY DESIGN

Principle 8: Public Amenities

Residents, including families with children, should have reasonable and safe access to local community services and recreational amenities. A high level of amenity for local residents is the direct result of supporting residential density that is appropriate to the site and context.

Objective 8.1: Local Amenities

Residents, including families with children, should have reasonable and safe access to local community services and recreational amenities.

Design Criteria

① Residential developments should be supported by a range of family-friendly local amenities, including:

- Schools;
- Multimodal transportation options;
- Retail and grocery stores;
- Community facilities (libraries, recreation centres, places of worship, community centres); and
- Parks, playgrounds, open spaces and natural areas.

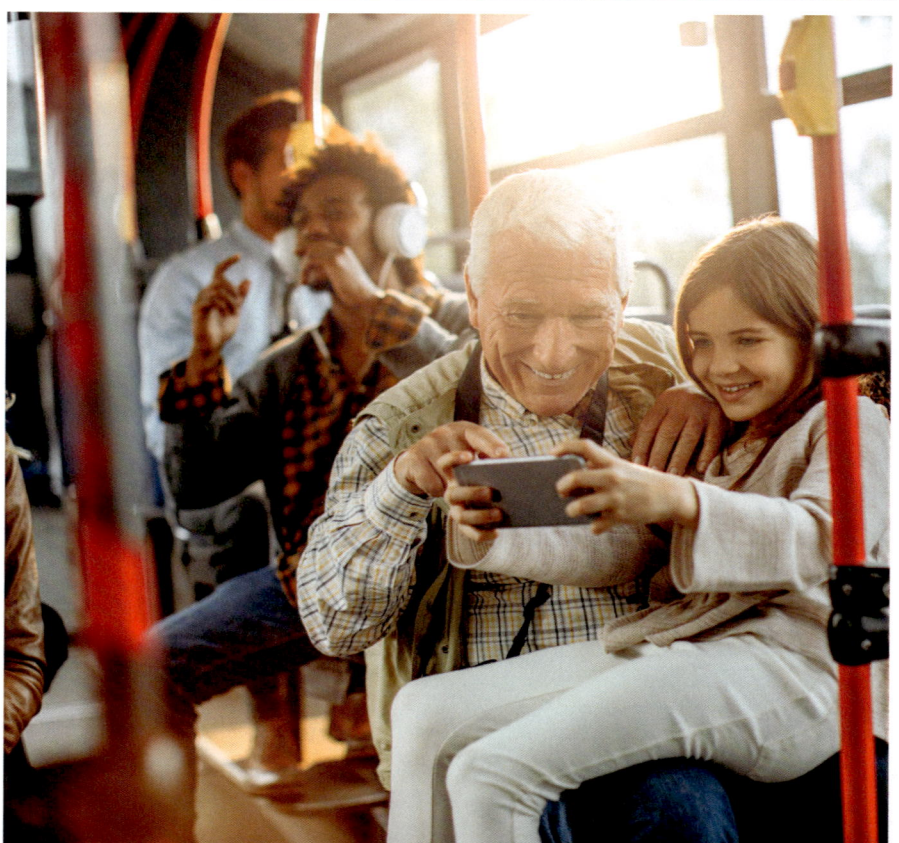

② Where local amenities, such as playgrounds or outdoor spaces, are not readily available within a close walking distance, additional on-site amenities should be provided.

③ Residential developments should be located within 800 m (10 minutes) safe walking distance to an elementary school, outdoor play area, child care facility, community centre, and grocery store.

④ Residential developments should be located within 400 m (5 minutes) safe walking distance to a playground and a public transit stop.

⑤ Older children should have access to natural areas, adventure playgrounds, recreation facilities, gathering spaces, and/or skate parks within 800 m (10 minutes) safe walking distance.

⑥ Opportunities for adolescents and teens should be provided, including underage nightlife and safe, inclusive places to hang out, such as shopping malls, cafés, and parks.

Facility	Catchment population	Reasonable walking distance at different gross densities[23,24]			
		Suburban Density 40 people/ha 17 units/ha	Mature Area Density 60 people/ha 25 units per ha	Urban Density 80 people/ha 45 unit/ha	Urban Centre 100 people/ha 85+ u/ha
Early childhood education or daycare	2,000	600 m	500 m	400 m	400 m
Elementary and Middle School	4,000	800 m	700 m	600 m	500 m
Local Secondary School	8,000	1,200 m	1,000 m	700 m	700 m
District Secondary School	16,000	1,500 m	1,200 m	1,000 m	1,000 m
Health Centre	10,000	1,200 m	1,000 m	900 m	800 m
Convenience Store	1,500	500 m	400 m	400 m	300 m
Library	6,000	1,000 m	800 m	700 m	600 m
Post Office	5,000	800 m	700 m	600 m	600 m
Community Centre	4,000	800 m	600 m	600 m	500 m
Local Centre	6,000	1,000 m	800 m	700 m	600 m
Grocery store	10,000	800 m	800 m	800 m	800 m
Leisure Centre	24,000	1,900 m	1,500 m	1,300 m	1,200 m
Transit every 10 min	25 units/ha	800 m	400 m	400 m	400 m
Café	800	800 m	800 m	400 m	200 m
Pharmacy	1,025	800 m	800 m	400 m	400 m
Clothing Store	2,000	1,500 m	1,500 m	800 m	400 m

Objective 8.2: Local Schools

Provide high-quality, convenient local schools.

Design Criteria

1 Explore opportunities to co-locate schools, parks, and child care facilities with new and infill residential development from the early stages of design and construction through partnerships and coordination between municipal and provincial levels of government, school boards, developers, and community groups.

2 New schools should be located near major transit routes, residential developments, and along safe walking routes.

3 School sites should be retained in mature communities to meet future enrollment or community space needs resulting from infill development.

Objective 8.3: Parks and Playgrounds

Parks, playgrounds, and open spaces provide outdoor social and recreation space, offering social, physical and mental health benefits for all residents.

Design Criteria

1 The design of parks and playgrounds should support discovery, adventure, imagination, and risk-taking through non-prescriptive design features.

2 Play environments and spaces for children should be designed to incorporate a range of spaces[25], including:

- spaces for thinking, experimenting, and discovering;
- spaces for taking moderate risks, facing challenges, and testing their physical abilities;
- spaces for spending time alone or with friends, away from overly-restrictive supervision, rules, and activities; and
- spaces to independently explore emotions and decisions within a flexible and responsive natural environment.

3 New parks and open spaces should be located on safe walking routes that minimize the number of intersections children need to cross to access them.

4 New parks and open spaces should be prioritized over

Design Criteria

1 Incorporate playful, child-friendly design elements into building design, public art, streetscapes, and landscaping that are fun, interactive, educational, musical, and/or colourful.

2 Discernible social centres - such as plazas, squares, parks, and greenspaces - should be located in close proximity to housing and be easily accessible via public transportation.

3 Incorporate landmarks into streetscapes and communities in order to support children's development of a cognitive map of their community.

4 Recognize that supporting active, walkable lifestyles is critical to reducing the overall carbon footprint of a city.

cash-in-lieu contributions and, where located off-site, should be located within a 5-10 minute walk (400 m – 800 m) of residential development.

5 Wherever possible, access to clean, safe public washrooms should be available year round.

6 Where possible, provide open Wi-Fi access to users in community gathering spaces.

Objective 8.4: Active and Playful Public Realm

Support the development of an active, animated, and playful public realm.

THE WAY OF THE WOONERF

"Woonerf" is a Dutch term meaning "Living Street." It is a design based on the premise that, without curbs, sidewalks, or other divisions between cars and people, vehicles will travel at a slower pace, thus enabling pedestrians and cyclists to take priority. These shared spaces are ornamented with trees, street furniture, play equipment, retail amenities, public art and, in some cases, parking.

There are four key features that are present in almost every woonerf. They include:

- Well-defined area boundaries and clear signage, including slow, clearly-articulated speed limits.

- Limited vehicle access, generally not exceeding 100 cars at peak times, and primarily limited to delivery vehicles, local traffic, and public transportation.

- Demarcation of space using paving stones, paint, stamped concrete, and permeable paving.

- Physical and gentle visual barriers to slow traffic and create social spaces, including trees and landscaping, planters, gently curved streets, public art, street furniture, and retail amenities. Care must be taken to ensure that these features do not obstruct driver vision and create dangerous areas for children.

A woonerf is designed as an integral part of the public realm. By enhancing the quality rather than the speed of life, a woonerf allows a city's circulation network to serve as a public living room. It is a space for socializing and slowing down, rather than merely passing though.

Principle 9: Transportation Networks

Safe walking and cycling routes support active living, connect child-specific destinations, and help mitigate real and/or perceived risk associated with independent mobility.

Objective 9.1: Safe Walking Routes

Walking routes should be safe, secure, and pleasant.

Design Criteria

① Linear walking distances to local community services and amenities should be reduced in areas where children must climb hills to reach their destination.

② Safe and secure walking routes to local schools, open spaces, playgrounds, and amenities should be provided, which are free from barriers such as the need to cross a major arterial road.

③ Signage should be used to indicate the presence of children on local streets.

④ Wayfinding signage should be designed to include colourful symbols, be understandable to children who cannot yet read, and be visible from a child's height.

Objective 9.2: Vehicle Access

Vehicle access is controlled and minimizes physical interactions.

Design Criteria

1. Driveways and lanes should be limited to one car width where they cross the public sidewalk.

2. Where a drive lane or parking structure services more than 3 vehicles, the driveway should be designed to ensure all vehicles leave the site in a forward direction.

3. Landscaping should be limited to 0.6 m in height and should carefully consider the visibility of children and pets.

4. Speed limits on residential streets should be limited to a maximum of 30 km/hr.

5. Landscaped curb extensions, shorter crossing distances, raised crosswalks, and crossing lights that consider children's walking speeds should be provided to support safe crossings;

6. Safe walking and cycling routes should be provided that connect child-specific destinations such as schools, community centres, libraries, parks, and playgrounds with residential developments.

Objective 9.3: Internal Streets and Laneways

Internal streets and laneways should be shared zones that prioritize pedestrian access.

Design Criteria

1. Residential streets, including internal lanes, mews, and woonerfs should prioritize pedestrians through reduced speed limits, varied surface materials, landscaping, and bollards.

2. All parts of a lane or internal street should be well-lit and visible from the public street to support safety.

3. Larger sites and courtyard developments should be served by well-designed, internal streets and lanes, rather than by long driveways.

4. Dwellings should address internal streets and lanes in the same way they would address a public street.

Objective 9.4: Busy Streets

Busy public streets should separate different modes of transportation for comfort, safety, and efficiency.

Design Criteria

1. Pedestrian, bicycle, and vehicle circulation should be physically separated for user safety.

2. Sidewalks and pedestrian pathways should be separated from vehicle lanes on busy roads by planted boulevards.

3. Bus and bicycle lanes should be given priority to support use, comfort, and efficiency.

4. Where possible, minimize curb radii and lane widths to reduce vehicle speed.

5. Adequate space for a bus stop should be provided.

Objective 9.5: Multimodal Pathways

Separated multimodal pathways should be provided to connect retail and amenity areas with residential communities through a network of green open spaces.

Design Criteria

1. High-traffic multimodal pathways should consider a separation of uses for pedestrians, bicycles, and mobility scooters.

2. Sidewalks and pedestrian pathways should be widened on routes leading to schools, daycares, and playgrounds to accommodate school-age children who are able to legally ride bicycles on the sidewalk.

ENDNOTES

1. City Lange, Alexandra. The Design of Childhood: How the Material World Shaped Independent Kids. New York: Bloomsbury Publishing Inc., 2018, p. 323.

2. Danenberg, Rosa, Vivian Doumpa, and Hans Karssenberg, eds. The City at Eye Level for Kids. Rotterdam: STIPO Publishing, 2018. www.thecityateyelevel.com (accessed June 14, 2019), p 21.

3. Lárusdóttir A. R. and Dederichs, A. "Evacuation Dynamics of Children: Walking Speeds, Flow Through Doors in Daycare Centres." Ph.D. Research, Technical University of Denmark, 2016, http://www.kias.org.uk/wp-content/uploads/2016/02/Walking-speed-children.pdf.

4. Edwards, C.P., Knoche, L., and Kumru, A.. "Play Patterns and Gender." Encyclopedia of Women and Gender, vol. 2. Ed. Judith Worrell (San Diego: Academic Press, 2001): 814. https://digitalcommons.unl.edu/cgi/viewcontent.cgi?article=1610&context=psychfacpub (accessed August 2, 2019)

5. Dunn, James R.. "Levels of Influence in the Built Environment on the Promotion of Healthy Child Development." Healthcare Quarterly, 15 Special Issue (4) July 2012: 32-37. doi:10.12927/hcq.2013.22944 (accessed October 25, 2019).

6. Kellner, Jessica. Housing Reclaimed: Sustainable Homes for Next to Nothing. Gabriola Island: New Society Publishers, 2011, p. 159.

7. Stanford Children's Health. "The Growing Child: School-Age." Lucille Packard Children's Hospital Stanford. https://www.stanfordchildrens.org/en/topic/default?id=the-growing-child-school-age-6-to-12-years-90-P02278 (accessed September 1, 2019).

8. Karsten, Lia. "Children's Use of Public Space: The Gendered World of the Playground" Childhood 10, iss. 4 (2003): 466. Accessed March 10, 2018. http://journals.sagepub.com/doi/abs/10.1177/0907568203104005

9. Edwards, C.P., Knoche, L., and Kumru, A.. "Play Patterns and Gender." Encyclopedia of Women and Gender, vol. 2. Ed. Judith Worrell (San Diego: Academic Press, 2001): 814. https://digitalcommons.unl.edu/cgi/viewcontent.cgi?article=1610&context=psychfacpub (accessed August 2,

2019)

10. Rose, Johnathan F.P. The Well-Tempered City: What Modern Science, Ancient Civilizations, and Human Nature Teach Us About the Future of Urban Life. New York: Harper Wave, 2016, p 315.

11. Lange, Alexandra. "The Moms Aren't Wrong: Why Planning for Children Would Make Cities Better for All." Alexandra Lange (blog), February 1, 2011. https://www.alexandralange.net/articles/12/the-moms-aren-t-wrong-why-planning-for-children-would-make-cities-better-for-all (accessed October 22, 2019), p 375.

12. For more information on Universal Design, please refer to the BC Building Access Handbook, CSA Standards, and Rick Hansen Foundation Guidelines.

13. City of Vancouver. High Density Housing for Families with Children Guidelines. July 13, 2016. https://vancouver.ca/files/cov/family-room-housing-mix-policy-for-rezoning-projects-2016-07-13.pdf (accessed October 3, 2019), p. 3.

14. City of Vancouver. Housing Design and Technical Guidelines, January 22, 2018. Version 9.7. https://vancouver.ca/files/cov/housing-design-and-technical-guidelines.pdf (accessed May 1, 2019). p.11

15. City of Vancouver. Housing Design and Technical Guidelines, January 22, 2018. Version 9.7. https://vancouver.ca/files/cov/housing-design-and-technical-guidelines.pdf (accessed May 1, 2019). p.11

16. City of Vancouver. High Density Housing for Families with Children Guidelines. July 13, 2016. https://vancouver.ca/files/cov/family-room-housing-mix-policy-for-rezoning-projects-2016-07-13.pdf (accessed October 3, 2019), p. 11.

17. Whitzman, Carolyn. (2017). Creating Child-Friendly Living Environments in Central Cities: Vertical Living Kids. doi: 10.1007/978-981-287-035-3_6, p. 9.

18. City of Vancouver. High Density Housing for Families with Children Guidelines. July 13, 2016. https://vancouver.ca/files/cov/family-room-housing-mix-policy-for-rezoning-projects-2016-07-13.pdf (accessed October 3, 2019), p. 6.

19. Whitzman, Carolyn. (2017). Creating Child-Friendly Living Environments in Central Cities: Vertical Living Kids. doi: 10.1007/978-981-287-035-3_6, p. 9.

20. Whitzman, Carolyn. (2017). Creating Child-Friendly Living Environments in Central Cities: Vertical Living Kids. doi: 10.1007/978-981-287-035-3_6, p. 9.

21. Alexander, Christopher, Sara Ishikawa, and Murray Silverstein. "Connected Play." *A*

Pattern Language: Towns, Buildings, Construction. Oxford University Press: New York, 1977, p. 342.

22. Register, Richard. *Ecocities: Rebuilding Cities in Balance with Nature*, Revised ed. Gabriola Island: New Society Publishers, 2006, p. 5.

23. Friedman, Avi. *Neighbourhood: Designing a Liveable Community.* Montréal: Véhicule Press, 2018, p 87.

24. City of Belfast. A Plan Fit for Children: Health at the Heart of the Local Development Plan, June 2017. https://www.belfasthealthycities.com/sites/default/files/publications/A%20Plan%20Fit%20for%20Children.pdf (accessed September 1, 2019)

25. Hyndman, Brendon. "Let them play! Kids need freedom from play restrictions to develop." The Conversation, May 23, 2019. https://theconversation.com/let-them-play-kids-need-freedom-from-play-restrictions-to-develop-117586 (accessed June 25, 2019).

26. Portland Child Friendly Housing p 5.

PART IV: PARTICIPATORY PLANNING WITH CHILDREN

> *"Where, after all, do universal human rights begin? In small places, close to home – so close and so small that they cannot be seen on any maps of the world … Unless these rights have meaning there, they have little meaning anywhere. Without concerted citizen action to uphold them close to home, we shall look in vain for progress in the larger world."*
> Eleanor Roosevelt

By challenging the notion that children are solely future citizens of a community – and acknowledging them as a unique and distinctive population of *current* citizens – planners, designers, and policy-makers can leverage opportunities to create communities that are more inclusive, playful, and livable for all residents. Children are increasingly being recognized as agents of change in their homes and communities, highlighting instances of social, financial, and physical inequities, concerns about the environmental sustainability of our planet, and questioning systemic issues such as racism, violence, and poverty[1].

The United Nations Convention on the Rights of the Child states that:

Parties shall assure to the child who is capable of forming his or her own views the right to express those views freely in all matters affecting the child, the views of the child being given due weight in accordance with the age and maturity of the child[2].

Effective participation and engagement with children and youth can help inform and strengthen decision-making at all stages of the planning and development process, from the early stages of community and neighbourhood planning to delivering individual projects.

While most participatory processes do not purposely seek to exclude children and families, consultation regarding land use, community planning, and individual developments tends to disproportionately consider input from adults, focusing on the needs of the caregiver, rather than the child. Children, in turn, are confined to discussions around playgrounds, skate parks, and, in some cases, child-specific programming. By expanding and diversifying the opportunities for consultation with children and youth, it is possible for local governments, planners, designers, developers, and policy-makers to support children's involvement in the design and management of their communities. As Harry Sheir notes, full and effective engagement with children and youth "requires an explicit commitment on the part of adults to share their power, that is to give some of it away[3]."

While children should not be pressured to take on unwanted or developmentally inappropriate responsibility, it is far more likely that adults will deny children desired opportunities for input and accountability than to force too much responsibility on them. Planners, designers, and policy makers are often hesitant to engage with children, believing that children will present them with unreasonable and unfeasible demands. In reality, however, the changes to a community which result from engaging with children may be deceptively simple. For example, children may identify a problematic crosswalk where vehicles don't yield, or a landscaped area that blocks their access to a park or playground. Children are vulnerable due to their size, age, and dependence on caregivers and therefore provide an excellent indication of how safe, inclusive, livable, and engaging a community is or is likely to be – if only we would listen to them.

Child-led participation
Children and youth lead participation based on their concerns and priorities. Children share responsibility for decision-making with adults.
Example: school strikes for climate.

Child-directed participation
Children direct and define engagement and participate in decision-making processes with the support of adults.
Example: child-led tours of local communities.

Child-focused participation
Adult-initiated engagement where children are consulted and involved in decision-making. Decisions are shared with children and children are helped to explore ways to achieve their objectives.
Example: design charrettes for local playgrounds.

Child-supported participation
Children are supported to develop a full understanding of the process and their opinions are taken seriously. This level of engagement is the minimum standard under the UN Convention on the Rights of the Child.
Example: surveys, interviews, and art activities.

Child-involved participation
Adults devise activities and invite children's participation in various, targeted engagement activities. Children may need to take initiative to express their opinion.
Example: consultation events hosted during school hours or at a local playground (with parent involvement).

Token child participation
Children may be asked for their input but do not participate in the decision-making process.
Example: Lego-building design workshop activities.

Symbolic child participation
Children are invited to participate in an event with their parents or caregivers. They may be asked for their opinion, but are not involved in decision-making.
Example: wearing t-shirts with project logos, or drawing pictures without further discussion or context.

Non-participation
Children are not supported to understand the issues.
Example: child care provided at consultation events, but children are not actively engaged; children are observed at a local playground.

11 AGE-APPROPRIATE CONSULTATION

Involving and engaging children, adolescents, and youth in designing and planning their communities offers a number of benefits that cross demographic, income, and geographic boundaries. Inclusive consultation and engagement processes allow children to build confidence, independence, and resilience. Moreover, participation in planning and local government processes allows children and youth the opportunity to develop a sense of social responsibility, hone their leadership skills, become engaged citizens, and understand civic opportunities as interactive processes, where community members collaborate to improve their shared environments and spaces. Embedding child and youth engagement activities at every stage of the planning and design process – from conception through implementation – can support children in making a significant contribution to their environment, their community, and their future.

Meaningful, child-friendly engagement must take into account children's developmental capabilities and interests, employing methods and processes that they find both engaging and relevant. This is particularly important for very young and school-age children who are unable to independently access public forums and who may have no other means of meaningfully influencing community decisions. For children, the responses from adult facilitators – including feedback about how their input has been considered and, at least partially, integrated – helps shape children's perceptions about the value of their opinions and influences whether they will continue to be engaged in civic processes as they age. But, just as different age groups have varying needs for design and environmental interventions, children and youth of different ages may have a variety of needs and expectations with respect to consultation and engagement. The following section will explore the needs of, and recommendations for, young children and their caregivers, school-age children, and adolescents.

Engagement with Young Children, Parents, and Caregivers (0-4 years old)
Urban environments can influence the way parents nurture and care for their children, support children's physical and emotional health, and enhance children's ability to develop resilience and independence. Early childhood environments are often focused on the home, local parks and playgrounds, healthcare facilities, and other places their caregivers visit with them. Infants and young children are often

found in close proximity to their parents and caregivers, therefore engaging with this demographic must also consider the needs of their caregivers. Additional effort may be required to support engagement with certain demographic groups, including low income, immigrant, lone parent, foster parent, and minority families.

Challenges to Engagement
- Expectant parents of all genders are often actively planning for the future and may feel overwhelmed by the emotional and mental load that accompanies preparing for the arrival of a child[4]. Engagement approaches should be straightforward and able to be completed without a significant ongoing time commitment.
- Infants and young children are limited in their capacity to articulate their needs and provide direct feedback as part of an engagement process, however preschool-age children are often able to communicate their likes and dislikes through imaginative play, art, and personal discussions.
- Caregivers can provide valuable information about specific, family-friendly needs as they navigate their communities accompanied by their children. For example, providing feedback about the availability of

change tables in both men's and women's washrooms, locations and styles of nursing facilities, navigating transit with strollers, the use of parks and public spaces, and paths of travel through neighbourhoods.
- Caregivers' attention may be divided when infants and young children are present and families often have limited time available. Engagement opportunities that are quick, flexible, allow movement, or can be completed remotely may provide higher levels of engagement than traditional public meeting and workshop structures.
- Toddlers and preschoolers may struggle to sit through events or activities, even if the activities are child-focused.
- Young children may be intimidated by unfamiliar adults due to differences in size, unclear expectations, and professional formalities. They may have limited vocabulary and may be unfamiliar with terms, drawing conventions, or symbols that adults regularly use.
- Parents and caregivers of young children may have difficulty overcoming fears about their children's future safety and independence in the community or city.

Strategies for Engagement
- Tailor activities to children's developmental stages: Educate facilitators on appropriate social and developmental expectations for toddlers and preschoolers. Understanding young children's need for movement, exploration, and play can help facilitators tailor activities and create environments that allow children to move, learn, play, and contribute in a positive and meaningful way.
- Go to families: Seek out opportunities to engage with families in public locations that are well-attended by children and their families. This can enable facilitators to decrease barriers to engagement, increase convenience, and reach community members who may not otherwise attend consultation events. These opportunities should be sensitive to the local context and should consider the type of activities that take place in the space, including any privacy considerations that may negatively impact participation[5].
- Incentivize participation: Consider incentives for families to encourage participation, especially by those facing significant barriers to inclusion. Participants may be provided with refreshments, parking or transit vouchers, child care, training and resources, or take-home activities for their children.
- Partner with child-focused organizations: Collaborate with organizations and institutions that offer programming for young children, such as daycares, libraries, museums, and preschools. Partnering with established service providers builds trust, supports ongoing participation, and increases children's comfort. Service providers and frontline staff may provide firsthand information about how people of all ages routinely access services or use spaces.
- Overcome fears: Reminding adults about their own childhood experiences can help them overcome fears about perceived community dangers relating to their children's access to the city.
- Excite and educate: Incorporate learning and participation into various aspects of planning, development, and daily life. Eye catching graphics, games and activities integrated into public spaces, little free libraries, and painted symbols on sidewalks can engage children and their families as they go about their day, while encouraging them to learn more about certain topics or areas.

- Tell the story of a community: Engage with toddlers and preschoolers through stories about their current experiences and imagined future of their communities. The facilitator may help children understand the project or location being discussed, but children should direct the plot and outcome of the story.
- See through a child's eyes: Young children often connect with places that are overlooked by adults. They may view a grassy knoll, tree, or boulder as play objects, landmarks, or imaginary worlds. Empower children to show or tell facilitators about the features and places they value through drawings, imaginative play, storytelling, and photographs.

Engaging with School-Age Children (5-12 years old)

Civic engagement has historically been focused on consultation activities between adults. Creating a truly child-centred engagement approach means connecting with children through activities which they find most compelling and comfortable. School-age children often have the ability to observe, communicate, and imagine their social and spatial needs. When given the independence and authority to draw their own conclusions and define how they want to express their input, children are often able to provide valuable insight into the strengths, issues, and needs of their communities. Notably, school-age children often include insects, animals, plants, natural elements, and groups of people in drawings and stories about their communities – elements that may be overlooked in conventional planning and design exercises.

Barriers to Engagement
- Families are frequently pressed for time and engagement events may conflict with extracurricular activities, play time, family time, or school activities. Ensure parents and caregivers understand the importance of including children's input into the future of their communities, both in terms of personal empowerment and the greater good.
- Allow families to drop in and leave workshops and engagement activities as necessary to accommodate extracurricular activities and commitments. Structuring activities into approximately 20 minute blocks allows families to participate as their schedule and interests permit[6].
- Adults seeking to engage with children may be concerned that children will present them with unreasonable demands or expectations. In some cases, what may seem like an unreasonable demand – for example, the ability to climb a school building or jump off a high wall – may, in fact, be a developmentally-appropriate expression of a child's spatial and physical needs. Children should be supported in seeking appropriate design responses to meet their physical, social, and developmental needs.
- Children may lack the vocabulary and lived experience to discuss their concerns about certain social issues. For example, poverty, homelessness, racism, and violence may be difficult for children to articulate when speaking about their experiences and communities.

Strategies for Engagement
- Co-facilitate activities: Partner with local schools, libraries, clubs, museums, and children's organizations to host events and support collaboration. Incorporating engagement activities into existing schedules and programs can ease the burden on families' time; however, engagement designed in this way should be optional and respectful of the primary activity. Schools can facilitate age-appropriate discussions

during classes to support their curriculum and help address children's questions about community issues, political processes, and how to get involved in civic processes.
- Let children lead: Children should be empowered and encouraged to identify their own needs and concerns without adult input or validation.
- Let children move: Support children's need for movement, play, and creative expression through a variety of activities and opportunities for input. Children can be given options of participating in discussions, creating drawings and photographs, or role playing, depending on their personalities and interests.
- Let children tell their story: Children can lead tours of their communities, alongside trusted caregivers, to provide facilitators, planners, and designers with an understanding of how they view the spaces around them. Similarly, children can take photographs of areas they like or dislike and should be encouraged to caption the photographs to explain which elements are of interest and why they took the photograph. Facilitators should understand that a child's interpretation of their photograph may be very different from an adult's.
- Support creative expression: Children can create maps, drawings, or

models of their communities. The elements children choose to emphasize or exclude can provide important information about their likes and dislikes. Children should be encouraged to describe or caption their artwork to record their observations and thoughts. If children's artwork is to be used in publications or as promotional materials, children should be given information about how their creations will be used and asked for their permission to share.
- Empower older children as leaders: Older children often take leadership roles seriously and can help younger children discuss their experiences of, and vision for, their community.
- Make participation fun: Incorporating games and role-playing into consultation activities can make engagement less intimidating and encourage honest and thoughtful feedback. Games and activities can help participants of all ages as they learn and experiment with different ideas and scenarios in a non-threatening environment.
- Transcribe results: Depending on the age of participants, facilitators may need to summarize or transcribe feedback. Facilitators should work with children to ensure that their ideas are properly represented and should report back to participants on how their ideas influenced the final project.

Engaging with Adolescents (10-19 years old)
Civic participation begins with understanding events, community dynamics, and community processes. For adolescents, community engagement activities provide an opportunity to understand municipal processes, engage with elected officials, and have an impact on the future of their communities. Early exposure to civic engagement opportunities has the potential to support young adults who are more likely to vote, engage with elected officials, and participate in community activism. Adolescents experience more spatial freedom than school-age children, but may still be restricted by inadequate transportation options, limited financial resources, time limitations, or spatial boundaries. Their emerging independence in the city offers a unique and critical perspective for planners and designers wishing to develop complete, inclusive communities.

Barriers to Engagement
- Adolescents, depending on their age, may not have complete autonomy over their time and schedule. School schedules, family responsibilities, and extracurricular activities may impede adolescents' abilities to attend regular meetings[7].
- Adolescents may be unfamiliar with, or intimidated by, formal engagement and meeting structures. For example, adolescents may be intimidated by speaking at Council meetings, public hearings, or other formal events and may prefer "teen only" opportunities for engagement.
- If activities are focused on younger adolescents, interest and engagement may decrease as teens "age out" of the targeted demographic group.
- Civic engagement may be seen as "uncool" and may interfere with other demands on an adolescent's time. Engagement activities need to clearly demonstrate the need for, and benefit from, participation in order to compete with other activities.
- Parents and adolescents may express concerns about privacy and data collection. Facilitators must ensure that all data collection – including online data collection – is undertaken anonymously in order to protect the identity and safety of children and their families.

Strategies for Engagement
- Go to them: Taking engagement opportunities to adolescents conveys the message that facilitators value their input and encourages more consistent

and convenient participation. Creating platforms for peer connection during engagement can provide opportunities for mutual learning and shift participation toward a youth-driven dialogue[8].
- Help adolescents find their voice: Adolescents often eagerly engage with creative and social means of expression, including photography, film making, creative expression, and site tours. If necessary, adolescents' creative abilities can be supported through prompts, constructive critiques, and exhibition opportunities, allowing them to find and develop their own unique, powerful, and meaningful voice.
- Use technology: Incorporating social media, online discussion forums, apps, and games into consultation processes can allow adolescents to contribute to discussions in a fun, engaging, and ongoing manner. However, while technology presents significant opportunities for data-sharing and collection, maintaining privacy and anonymity must be a priority to ensure the safety of all participants.
- Provide opportunities for praxis: Praxis refers to the thoughtful reflection and application of skills and knowledge to bring about change. Adolescents should be supported as they develop and test their ideas throughout a project's phases. At a minimum, adolescents should have

the opportunity to provide input and receive feedback about how their input was addressed in the final project.
- Eliminate barriers: Ensure that meetings are held outside of school hours at venues that are easily accessible on foot or via public transportation. Be conscientious about any hidden fees for participation, such as entrance fees, parking and transit costs, or expectations to purchase refreshments at the venue.
- Partner with local schools: Schools provide a unique opportunity for planners, designers, and policy-makers to give real-world context to curriculum. Partnering with schools and empowering students to understand and become involved in civic processes helps support their future as engaged citizens.
- Support and encourage participation: Participation in formal planning processes can be overwhelming for participants of any age. To support and encourage the participation of adolescents, it may be necessary to brief Boards, Councils, and staff members about the importance of youth participation. Adolescents may require additional time, support, or encouragement to voice their opinions, particularly in formal or crowded proceedings.
- Adapt physical spaces: Few adolescents are accustomed to sitting around a boardroom table. While this setup can provide an empowering experience, it can also be intimidating. Meeting spaces should be designed to support both group activities and more intimate break-out conversations in order to give participants the flexibility to participate in a manner that is most comfortable for them.
- Support co-learning: In ongoing consultation activities, participants may need to undertake further research to increase their understanding of a particular topic. Rather than providing solutions or doing the research for adolescents, facilitators can encourage a co-learning process where adolescents seek out their own information and share it with their peers.
- Encourage accountability: Adolescents should be encouraged to contact facilitators, attend meetings, and participate in workshops independently. Supporting adolescents to take initiative will help ensure that participants are engaged and invested as partners throughout the project[9].
- Make engagement reciprocal: Effective community engagement processes help participants understand that their time and efforts are worthwhile.

Adolescents who are able to see the impact of their contributions are more likely to remain engaged in their communities – from attending public meetings to voting or running for an elected position – as they enter into adulthood.

Children: Our Present, Our Future

Empowering children to actively participate in planning their communities supports the development of an equitable, active, and engaged society. Children engage with their environments differently than adults do, often giving special meaning to the insects, animals, and landscapes that surround them. To limit children's contributions is to miss the opportunity for children to actively participate in society, thereby perpetuating a system where the community is passed down to – rather than co-created with – children.

Children are not solely the stewards of our future cities; they are citizens today, with valid and valuable perspectives, experiences, and opinions about their communities and futures. By placing children's rights at the forefront of the planning process, local governments and policy-makers can support the development of communities and environments that are inclusive, sustainable, and livable for all – if only we listen to them.

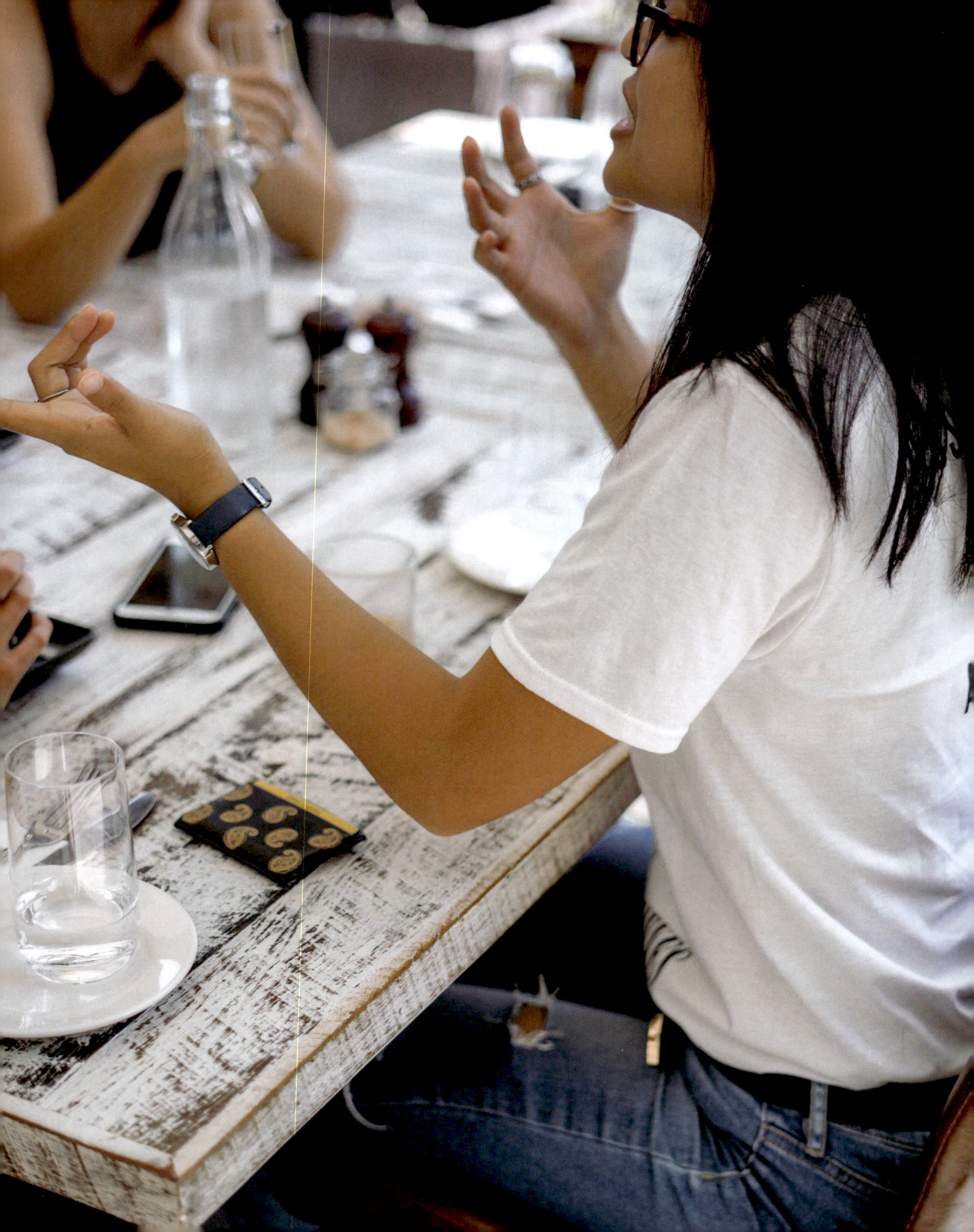

ENDNOTES

1. Bishop, Kate and Linda Corkery, eds. Designing Cities with Children and Young People: Beyond Playgrounds and Skate Parks. New York: Routledge, 2017, p. 32.

2. United Nations Office of the High Commissioner. Convention on the Rights of the Child. Resolution of the General Assembly. November 20, 1989. https://www.ohchr.org/en/professionalinterest/pages/crc.aspx (accessed July 4, 2019), Article 12.1.

3. Shier, Harry. "Pathways to Participation: Openings, Opportunities and Obligations." Children & Society 15(2):107-117 (March 2001). doi: 10.1002/chi.617 (accessed November 1, 2019), p. 115.

4. 880 Cities, Bernard Van Leer Foundation, and Urban 95. 2017. "Building Better Cities with Young Children and Families." bernardvanleer.org https://bernardvanleer.org/app/uploads/2017/10/BvLF-8-80-Cities-Report-Final.pdf (accessed May 12, 2019), p 11.

5. 880 Cities, Bernard Van Leer Foundation, and Urban 95. 2017. "Building Better Cities with Young Children and Families." bernardvanleer.org https://bernardvanleer.org/app/uploads/2017/10/BvLF-8-80-Cities-Report-Final.pdf (accessed May 12, 2019), p 16.

6. Derr, Victoria, Louise Chawla, Mara Mintzer, Debra Flanders Cushing, and Willem Van Vliet. "A City for All Citizens: Integrating Children and Youth from Marginalized Populations into City Planning." Buildings. 3, 482-505 (July 2013); doi:10.3390/buildings3030482 (accessed September 2, 2019, p. 498.

7. LoIacono, Marni, Carolyn Rodgers, Ellen Silver, Jamie Sclafane, and Laurie Bauman. "Engaging and sustaining adolescents in community-based participatory research: structuring a youth-friendly community-based participatory research environment." Family and Community Health. 2015;38(1):22–32. doi:10.1097/FCH.0000000000000057 (accessed June 3, 2019).

8. Derr, Victoria, Louise Chawla, Mara Mintzer, Debra Flanders Cushing, and Willem Van Vliet. "A City for All Citizens: Integrating Children and Youth from Marginalized Populations into City Planning." Buildings. 3, 482-505

(July 2013); doi:10.3390/buildings3030482 (accessed September 2, 2019), p. 500.

9. LoIacono, Marni, Carolyn Rodgers, Ellen Silver, Jamie Sclafane, and Laurie Bauman. "Engaging and sustaining adolescents in community-based participatory research: structuring a youth-friendly community-based participatory research environment." Family and Community Health. 2015;38(1):22–32. doi:10.1097/FCH.0000000000000057 (accessed June 3, 2019).

: COMMUNITY
ASSESSMENT
CHECKLIST

PREPARATION

TASK	CHECK COMPLETED	STATUS (note activities conducted toward task completion, barriers, etc.)
Community assessment checklist template reviewed. Approach and purpose has been discussed with planning officer.	☐	
Identified individuals to assist with the community assessment process.	☐	
Consider forming a community assessment workgroup.	☐	
Development of a reporting structure and schedule.	☐	

INCLUSIVENESS OF THE ASSESSMENT

Check the boxes below to indicate representatives from key sectors that have been included in the assessment. Check boxes indicating level of involvement have been included in order to gauge levels of participation.

1. Children and caregivers from the community are involved in the assessment process.

   Check all that apply:
   ☐ Helped conduct the assessment
   ☐ Data collected from them
   ☐ Helped review the findings

   Notes:

2. Representatives from the child care sector are involved in the assessment process.

   Check all that apply:
   ☐ Helped conduct the assessment
   ☐ Data collected from them
   ☐ Helped review the findings

   Notes:

3. Representatives from the School Board are involved in the assessment process.

   Check all that apply:
   ☐ Helped conduct the assessment
   ☐ Data collected from them
   ☐ Helped review the findings

   Notes:

INCLUSIVENESS OF THE ASSESSMENT (CONTINUED)

Check the boxes below to indicate representatives from key sectors that have been included in the assessment. Check boxes indicating level of involvement have been included in order to gauge levels of participation.

4. Professionals who address issues related to family services, public health, and/or community services are involved in the assessment process.

   Check all that apply:
   ☐ Helped conduct the assessment
   ☐ Data collected from them
   ☐ Helped review the findings

   Notes:

5. A dedicated CPTED professional has been involved in the assessment process.

   Check all that apply:
   ☐ Helped conduct the assessment
   ☐ Data collected from them
   ☐ Helped review the findings

   Notes:

DATA ANALYSIS AND DISTRIBUTION

Check the boxes below to indicate analysis and distribution of the information collected. Check boxes indicating degree of distribution have been included in order to support monitoring and evaluation of policies and programs.

6. Results of community assessment have been analyzed, collated, and compared to baseline figures.

   Check all that apply:
   ☐ First assessment: baseline prepared
   ☐ Report prepared presenting baseline and current conditions (if different)
   ☐ Relevant policies and programs are identified

7. Results of community assessment have been widely shared and distributed and comments have been collated based on feedback from the different audiences it has been shared with.

   Check all that apply:
   ☐ Available on the municipal website
   ☐ Shared with news agencies
   ☐ Presented at a public open house

8. Results of community assessment have been presented to Council as part of a policy or program update.

   Check all that apply:
   ☐ Presented to Council for information as a baseline
   ☐ Presented to Council as part of a policy or program update

COMMUNITY ASSESSMENT CHECKLIST

Observer: _____

Date: _____

Community: _____

Community Segment: _____

Plans in Effect (OCP, Neighbourhood Plan, zoning overlay, etc): _____

Temperature: _____

Weather (rain, snow, frost, fog, etc): _____

OUTDOOR SPACES AND BUILDINGS

	INDICATOR	MEASURE
1	Public areas are clean and pleasant. Green spaces and outdoor seating are sufficient in number, well-maintained and safe.	**Street Trees** Street trees are planted at regular intervals along public sidewalks. ☐ Every 6-12 m ☐ On one side of the street ☐ On both sides of the street ☐ Street trees are well-maintained and trimmed to at least 2.4 m clear height. ☐ Shrubs do not exceed 0.6 m in height around children's play areas, parking areas, and along pedestrian pathways. **Benches** ☐ Benches are provided every 100-400 m. ☐ Benches are stable. ☐ Benches have a minimum seat height of 450 mm (18"). ☐ Benches provide colour contrast with the ground. ☐ Benches are clean and undamaged. ☐ Bench count: _____ **Public Spaces** ☐ Pedestrian pathways in park areas are a minimum of 1,500 mm in width. ☐ Recreational shared-use pathways are at least 3,500 mm in width. ☐ Areas of open space separate active areas from places to sit and observe through the use of pathways and landscaping elements. ☐ Outdoor fitness equipment is provided in parks and adjacent to public buildings. ☐ Snow is cleared in winter and anti-slip agents are used. ☐ New developments are oriented to maximize sunlight penetration into public spaces and impede prevailing winds. **Air Quality Health Index Value (Environment Canada)** ☐ Low Risk ☐ Moderate Risk ☐ High Risk ☐ Very High Risk

OUTDOOR SPACES AND BUILDINGS (CONTINUED)

	INDICATOR	MEASURE
2	Pavements are well-maintained, free of obstructions and reserved for pedestrians. Pavements are non-slip, are wide enough for strollers and have dropped curbs to road level. Cycle paths are separate from pavements and other pedestrian walkways.	**Sidewalks** Sidewalks are continuous and unobstructed. ☐ One side of the street ☐ Both sides of the street ☐ Sidewalks are a minimum of 1,500 mm in width in residential areas. ☐ Sidewalks are a minimum of 2,500 mm in width along retail and mixed-use streets. **Curb Cuts** ☐ Curb cuts are present. ☐ Curb cuts have grooves or bumps. ☐ Curb cut have a colour or material contrast with sidewalk. ☐ Curb cuts have a broad apron. ☐ Curb cuts align with crosswalks. **Materials** Sidewalks are constructed from: ☐ Broom-finished concrete ☐ Asphalt ☐ Brick ☐ Gravel or dirt ☐ Cobblestone **Condition** ☐ Sidewalks are level and in good condition. ☐ Sidewalks are cracked or uneven. ☐ Sidewalks are obstructed by street furniture, utility poles, or street trees. ☐ Sidewalks are under repair. ☐ Sidewalks are visually-consistent in terms of colour and texture. **Access** ☐ Street furniture, utility poles, and street trees are located in a "furniture zone" outside the path of travel. ☐ Cycle paths are provided that are separate from pedestrian walkways. ☐ Public sidewalks, bus stops, and curb ramps are not subject to flooding.
3	Outdoor safety is promoted by good street lighting, adjacent homes, and community education.	**Lighting** ☐ Streets are evenly lit. ☐ Parking areas are open, well-lit, and provide a clear path to entrances. **Eyes on the Street** ☐ Residential buildings have porches or balconies that face the street. ☐ Residential and commercial doors and windows face the street. ☐ Outdoor dining areas are located on or overlook the street.

OUTDOOR SPACES AND BUILDINGS (CONTINUED)

	INDICATOR	MEASURE

4	Pedestrian crossings are sufficient in number and safe for people of different ages and levels of ability, with nonslip markings, visual and audio cues and adequate crossing times.
	
	Drivers give way to pedestrians at intersections and pedestrian crossings.
		Crosswalks
		☐ Pedestrian crosswalks are marked:
		  ☐ Painted Lines
		  ☐ Zebra Stripes
		  ☐ Raised Crosswalk
		  ☐ Alternative Paving (brick, coloured concrete)
		  ☐ Pedestrian Signals
		  ☐ Pedestrian Crossing Sign
		  ☐ Unmarked
		☐ Marked pedestrian crosswalks are equipped with lighting, reflective crossing signs, and reflective surface markings.
		☐ Crossing times require a walking speed of no more than 1.0 m/s.
		
		Block Sizes
		☐ Block sizes do not exceed 150 m in length.
		☐ Mid-block crossings are provided on blocks greater than 100 m in length.

5	Buildings are well-signed outside and inside.	**Signage** ☐ Signage is clear and well-lit, with large, high-contrast lettering. ☐ Signage is visible from a child's height or a seated position. ☐ Signage includes images and is understandable for children who cannot yet read.
6	Public toilets outdoors and indoors are sufficient in number, clean, well-maintained and accessible.	**Public Toilets** ☐ Public toilets are located in community parks, along waterfronts, in commercial areas, and areas with moderate to large numbers of pedestrians. ☐ Public toilets are clean and well-maintained. ☐ Public toilets are accessible for strollers and wheelchairs. ☐ Change tables are provided.

HOUSING

INDICATOR	MEASURE

	Services and Amenities
	Residential developments are located within 400-800 m of retail and service centres (check all that apply):
	☐ School
	☐ Playground
	☐ Library
	☐ Community Centre
	☐ Grocery Store
	☐ Pharmacy
	☐ Religious Institution
	☐ Restaurant
	☐ Bank
	☐ Medical Clinic
	☐ Convenience Store
	☐ Other:
	☐ Low density neighbourhoods permit small, retail and commercial uses at designated locations.
	☐ Dwelling units are located a maximum of 400 m from open spaces.
7 Sufficient, affordable housing is available in areas that are safe and close to services and the rest of the community.	**Housing Types**
	A range of building types are available (check all that apply):
	☐ Low-rise Multi-unit (less than 5 storeys) with 2 bedrooms
	☐ Low-rise Multi-unit (less than 5 storeys) with 3+ bedrooms
	☐ High-rise Multi-unit (greater than 5 storeys) with 2 bedrooms
	☐ High-rise Multi-unit (greater than 5 storeys) with 3+ bedrooms
	☐ Duplex, Triplex and Fourplex
	☐ Row House or Townhouse
	☐ Single-detached
	☐ Garden and Laneway Suites
	☐ Secondary Suites
	☐ Manufactured Home
	☐ Tiny House
	☐ Other:
	Housing Tenure and Affordability
	There are a range of housing tenures available (check all that apply):
	☐ Ownership
	☐ Rental
	☐ Co-operative
	☐ Cohousing
	☐ The majority of families in the community are spending no more than 30% of their income on housing (Statistics Canada).
	☐ A minimum of 25% of units have two or more bedrooms.
	☐ A minimum of 10% of units have three or more bedrooms.

HOUSING (CONTINUED)

	INDICATOR	MEASURE
8	Sufficient and affordable home maintenance and support services are available. Home modification options and supplies are available and affordable.	**Maintenance** ☐ Dwelling units appear to be well-maintained. ☐ Properties appear to be well-maintained. ☐ A list of local service providers is available through the local business association or local government office.

9	Housing is well-constructed and provides safe and comfortable shelter from the weather.
	
	Public and commercial rental housing is clean, well-maintained and safe.
	
	Sufficient and affordable housing for families, with appropriate services, is provided locally.
		Environmental Design
		☐ New developments are oriented to maximize sunlight penetration.
		☐ Roof designs prevent falling ice, snow, and discharge of downspouts onto entrances and walkways.
		☐ Ramps and stairs are protected from ice and snow by a roof or canopy.
		☐ Dwelling entrances are protected from rain, ice, and snow by a roof or canopy.
		
		Neighbourliness
		☐ Fences along front property lines are no higher than 1.2 m.
		☐ Dwelling units incorporate front porches, balconies, and landscaped areas that face the public street.
		☐ Developments include 20-30 homes per building, up to a maximum of 70 children in one project.
		☐ Family units are grouped together on lower floors near communal areas.
		
		Legibility
		☐ Entrances to dwellings are easy to identify from the street.
		☐ Dwelling units have clear addresses and distinguishable features.
		
		Private and Semi-private Amenities
		Private open space is provided for every dwelling, with a minimum size of:
		    ☐ 8 m^2 for a one bedroom or studio
		    ☐ 12 m^2 for a two bedroom
		    ☐ 16 m^2 for a three bedroom
		☐ Any private balcony or outdoor space measures at least 1.8 m x 2.7 m.
		☐ At least 25% of private outdoor space is covered for weather protection.
		☐ Each development contains an indoor multipurpose room large enough to accommodate 40% of the building's anticipated adult population.
		☐ Outdoor courtyard spaces are fully open to the sky.
		☐ At least 1.0 m^2 of outdoor place space is allocated for preschool children and 1.5 m^2 per bedroom of play space is allocated for school age children, with a minimum area of 85 m^2.

TRANSPORTATION

	INDICATOR	MEASURE
10	Complete and accessible information is provided to users about routes, schedules and special needs facilities. All city areas and services are accessible by public transport, with good connections and well-marked routes and vehicles. Specialized transportation is available for persons with disabilities.	**Services and Amenities** ☐ Transit signage is clear and well-lit, with large, high-contrast lettering and graphics. ☐ Signage includes colourful symbols and is understandable to children who cannot yet read. ☐ Signage is visible from a child's height. ☐ Collector routes and on-demand options (school buses) are available.
11	Drivers stop at designated stops and beside the curb to facilitate boarding and wait for passengers to be seated before driving off. Transport stops and stations are conveniently located, accessible, safe, clean, well-lit and well-marked, with adequate seating and shelter.	**Transit Stop Locations** ☐ Transit stops are spaced 200-300 m apart in business districts and urban centres. ☐ Transit express routes stop at major family-friendly destinations. ☐ Transit stop spacing in rural areas should not exceed 400 m. ☐ Transit stops are provided adjacent to schools, playgrounds, community recreation centres, grocery stores, medical centres and locations frequently visited by children and their caregivers. ☐ Transit stops are located with level access to a majority of shops and services. **Transit Stop Amenities** ☐ Transit stops provide seating that is a minimum of 450 mm (18") in height. ☐ Transit stops provide shelter from the elements.

TRANSPORTATION (CONTINUED)

	INDICATOR	MEASURE
13	Roads are well-maintained, with covered drains and good lighting. Traffic flow is well-regulated. Roadways are free of obstructions that block drivers' vision. Traffic signs and intersections are visible and well-placed.	**Street Characteristics** ☐ Number of lanes: _____ ☐ One-way ☐ Two-way ☐ Bicycle Lane ☐ Dead end or Cul-de-sac **Street Condition** ☐ Good ☐ Adequate, but with some concerns for children's safety ☐ Poor
14	Parking and drop-off areas are safe, sufficient in number and conveniently located. Priority parking and drop-off spots for parents and people with special needs are available and respected.	**Parking Location** ☐ Designated accessible parking is located within 60 m of dwelling and retail entrances. ☐ On-street accessible parking is located immediately adjacent to curb cuts, ramps, or driveways. ☐ Parking leads to dwelling and retail entrances through a single, level pathway. ☐ Where more than 3 vehicles are serviced by one lane, the driveway is designed so vehicles leave the site in a forward direction.
	Progress toward child-friendly transportation goals and objectives.	**Progress** ☐ Significant Progress (>75%) ☐ Moderate Progress (50-75%) ☐ Initial Progress (25-50%) ☐ Progress Needed (<25%) Notes:

APPENDIX B
BUILDING ASSESSMENT CHECKLIST

BUILDING ASSESSMENT CHECKLIST: FAMILY-FRIENDLY DWELLING

	FEATURE	MEASURE
1	Access	**Building Entrance** ☐ Dwelling offers no-step entrances at all building entrances. 　☐ Front entrance 　☐ Side entrance 　☐ Rear entrance 　☐ Garage entrance **Site and Pathway** ☐ Site grading has been designed to support a no-step entry. ☐ Site grading does not exceed 1:20. ☐ An accessible pathway from the public sidewalk to the residential development is provided and is a minimum of 1,500 mm in width. ☐ The pathway is designed with a stable, firm, and slip-resistant surface. **Entrance** ☐ The entrance landing has a level area of at least 1,500 mm x 1,500 mm. ☐ The entrance is sheltered from rain and snow by an overhang.
2	Circulation	**Internal Circulation** ☐ The entrance has a minimum area of 4m^2 with a minimum width of 1.5 m to accommodate 4 people and/or a stroller inside the unit. ☐ Hallways have a minimum width of 1,500 mm. ☐ A turning radius of 1,500 mm is provided at all doors. ☐ All rooms provide a turning radius of 1,500 mm. ☐ A maximum of 12 units are serviced by one corridor.
3	Doors and Doorways	**Doors** ☐ All doorways provide a minimum 860 mm clear opening. ☐ All exterior doorways provide a minimum 915 mm clear opening. ☐ Two door viewers are provided at the unit entry at 1,050 mm and at 1,520 mm. ☐ All doors are equipped with lever-type hardware. **Thresholds** ☐ All doorways have flush thresholds not exceeding 13 mm in height.

BUILDING ASSESSMENT CHECKLIST: FAMILY-FRIENDLY DWELLING (CONTINUED)

	FEATURE	MEASURE
4	Bathrooms	**Main Floor Bathroom** ☐ At least one three-piece bathroom is located on the main level. **Bathroom Features** ☐ Bathroom has either a pocket door or an outward-swinging door. ☐ Bathroom has a turn radius of at least 1,500 mm and can accommodate a parent or caregiver helping a child. **Bathroom Fixtures** ☐ Lever-type faucets are installed. ☐ A bathtub is provided in at least one bathroom. ☐ Mirror is positioned at a height that is visible to a child.
5	Bedrooms	**Main Floor Bedroom/Flex Room** ☐ Dens are designed with sufficient area to support an "inboard" bedroom. ☐ Rooms are designed for 24 hour use. **Bedroom Features** ☐ Bedrooms offer a turn radius of 1,500 mm. ☐ The minimum area of any room is 10 m² and at least one bedroom has a minimum area of 12 m². ☐ Bedrooms have a minimum length and width of 3 m. ☐ Closet shelves and rods are height-adjustable.
6	Kitchen	**Layout** ☐ Kitchen offers a turn radius of 1,500 mm. ☐ Kitchen has a continuous counter between the stove and the sink. ☐ Kitchen has sightlines to the living room or play areas. **Features and Fixtures** ☐ Lever-type faucets are installed. ☐ Task lighting is installed at sink, stove, and work areas. ☐ Pull-out work boards are installed at 810 mm above the floor.
7	Laundry and Storage	**Laundry** ☐ Side-by-side laundry is located on the ground floor. ☐ A minimum of 16 linear metres of outdoor space per dwelling is provided for clothes drying. ☐ Sufficient space is provided to store 3 bicycles per household. ☐ Bicycle parking includes space for cargo bikes. ☐ A minimum of 5.7 m³ of storage should be provided per unit, with at least 50% inside the dwelling.
8	Patio/Balcony	**Patio/Balcony** ☐ Patio/balcony has a minimum of 800 mm clear doorway opening. ☐ Patio/balcony access has a threshold of no more than 13 mm. ☐ Patio/balcony offers a turn radius of 1,500 mm. ☐ Patio/balcony has a weather-protective covering.

BUILDING ASSESSMENT CHECKLIST: FAMILY-FRIENDLY DWELLING (CONTINUED)

	FEATURE	MEASURE
9	Flooring	**Flooring** ☐ Flooring is slip-resistant and non-glare. ☐ Carpet is firm, low-pile with cut pile of 13 mm or less. ☐ Walls and floors are insulated to muffle sound of at least 55 db.
10	Windows	**Windows** ☐ Window sill height does not exceed 750 mm above floor. ☐ Window opening and locking mechanisms are no more than 1,170 mm above the floor. ☐ No part of a habitable room is more than 8 m from a window. ☐ Windows on upper floors do not swing or tilt outwards. ☐ Window hardware are easily operated with one hand and require little to no force. ☐ Living rooms have receive direct or indirect sunlight for at least 2 hours per day during the winter solstice.
11	Outlets and Switches	**Outlets and Switches** ☐ Telephone jacks are provided in all bedrooms. ☐ Duplex outlets are located beside telephone jacks. ☐ Light switches are located between 1,050 mm and 1,220 from the floor. ☐ Outlets are equipped with tamper-resistant child safety features. ☐ Electrical outlets, cable outlets, and telephone jacks are located no less than 450 mm from the floor. **Fixtures** ☐ All switches are rocker or paddle-type. ☐ Combination light switch and outlets are located at room entrances. ☐ One outlet in each bedroom is wired to a three-way switch at the room entrance. ☐ All bedrooms are connected to the fire alarm.
12	Legibility	**Visibility and Colour Contrast** ☐ Colour-contrasting signage is used for unit numbers. ☐ Colour-contrasting exit doors are provided.

APPENDIX C
HYPOTHETICAL
PROFORMAS

Sample Developer's Proforma - All figures are Hypothetical for Illustrative Purposes Only
Housing Development

Major Assumptions (shading indicates figures that are inputs; unshaded cells are formulas)

Market Houses

Revenue and Value
Average Sales Price Per Sq. Ft.	$650	per sq.ft. of net saleable residential space

Site and Building Size
Site Size	0.28	acres or	12,301 sq. ft.
Site Frontage	32.07	meters	
Total Assumed Density	0.50	FAR	
Total Floorspace	6,151	sq.ft.	
Gross Residential Floorspace	6,151	sq.ft.	
Net Residential Floorspace	6,151	sq.ft.	
Average Gross Unit Size	3,075	sq.ft.	
Average Net Unit Size	3,075	sq.ft.	100.0% of gross area
Number of Units	2	Houses	7 units per acre
Total Parking Stalls	4	Parking Spaces	

Land Related Costs
Land Acquisition Cost	$1,179,566
Property Transfer Tax	$21,591
Financing Costs on Land Acquistion	$73,723

Construction Costs
Water, Storm, Sanitary Connections (Includes water meter, if applicable)	$50,000	
Hard Construction Costs	$200	per gross sq.ft.
Landscaping	$61,505	$15/sq ft for 30% of site area
Soft Costs	12.0%	of hard costs, servicing, landscaping
Contingency on Hard and Soft Costs	5.0%	of hard and soft costs
Post Construction Holding Costs	$3,000	$500/unit for 50% of units for 6 months
Interim Financing on Construction Costs	5.0%	on 50% of hard and soft costs, assuming 1.25 year construction period
Financing Fees	1.50%	of hard and soft costs

Other Costs and Allowances
Rezoning Costs	$0	Currently zoned for single family residential
Marketing on Residential	3.0%	of gross residential revenue
Sales Costs and Commissions	3.0%	of gross residential revenue
Residential Property Taxes	$27,305	0.683% of assessed value

Analysis

Revenue
Gross Sales Revenue	$3,997,825
Less Marketing and Commissions	$239,870
Net Sales Revenue	$3,757,956

Land Related Costs
Land Acquisition Cost	$1,179,566
Property Transfer Tax	$21,591
Financing Costs on Land Acquistion	$73,723
Subtotal - Land and Related Costs	$1,274,880

Construction Costs
Rezoning Costs	$0
On-Site Servicing (Upgrade of Adjacent Roads/Sidewalks/etc)	$0
Water, Storm, Sanitary Connections	$50,000
Cost of Underground Parking	$0
Hard Construction Costs	$1,230,100
Landscaping	$61,505
Soft Costs	$154,993
Contingency on Hard and Soft Costs	$74,830
Residential DCC Charge	$0
Property Taxes	$27,305
Post Construction Holding Costs	$3,000
Interim Financing on Construction Costs	$49,960
Financing Fees/Costs	$23,571
Subtotal - Construction Costs	$1,675,264

Developer's Profit	$807,811
Profit Margin on Revenues/Value	20.2%
Profit Margin on Costs	25.3%

Notes:
Soft costs allow for permits, design, engineering, legal, survey, insurance, project management, consultants, warranties, deficiencies, misc.

APPENDIX C | 143

Sample Developer's Proforma - All figures are Hypothetical for Illustrative Purposes Only
Townhouse Development

Major Assumptions (shading indicates figures that are inputs; unshaded cells are formulas)

Market Townhouses

Revenue and Value
Average Sales Price Per Sq. Ft.	$750	per sq.ft. of net saleable residential space
Average Sales Price Per Sq. Ft. for Affordable Units	$525	per sq.ft. of net saleable affordable residential space

Site and Building Size
Site Size	0.28	acres or	12,301 sq. ft.
Site Frontage	32.07	meters	
Total Assumed Density	0.70	FAR	
Total Floorspace	8,611	sq.ft.	
Gross Residential Floorspace	8,611	sq.ft.	
Net Residential Floorspace	8,611	sq.ft.	
Average Gross Unit Size	1,435	sq.ft.	
Average Net Unit Size	1,435	sq.ft.	100.0% of gross area
Number of Units	6	units or	21 units per acre
Total Parking Stalls	12	stalls	2 stalls per unit

Land Related Costs
Land Acquisition Cost	$1,179,566
Property Transfer Tax	$21,591
Financing Costs on Land Acquistion	$73,723

Construction Costs
On-Site Servicing (3)	$80,175	$2,500/m frontage
Water, Storm, Sanitary Connections (Includes water meter, if applicable)	$50,000	
Cost of Underground Parking	$600,000	$50,000 per spot
Hard Construction Costs	$230	per gross sq.ft.
Landscaping	$92,258	$15/sq ft for 50% of site area
Soft Costs	12.0%	of hard costs, servicing, landscaping
Contingency on Hard and Soft Costs	5.0%	of hard and soft costs
Residential DCC Charge	$26,263	$3.05/per square foot
Post Construction Holding Costs	$9,000	$500/unit for 50% of units for 6 months
Interim Financing on Construction Costs	5.0%	on 50% of hard and soft costs, assuming 1.25 year construction period
Financing Fees	1.50%	of hard and soft costs

Other Costs and Allowances
Rezoning Costs	$10,000	
Marketing on Residential	3.0%	of gross residential revenue
Sales Costs and Commissions	3.0%	of gross residential revenue
Residential Property Taxes	$44,108	0.683% of assessed value

Analysis

Revenue
Gross Multi-family Sales Revenue	$6,458,025
Less Marketing and Commissions	$387,482
Net Sales Revenue	$6,070,544

Land Related Costs
Land Acquisition Cost	$1,179,566
Property Transfer Tax	$21,591
Financing Costs on Land Acquistion	$73,723
Subtotal - Land and Related Costs	$1,274,880

Construction Costs
Rezoning Costs	$10,000
On-Site Servicing (Upgrade of Adjacent Roads/Sidewalks/etc)	$80,175
Water, Storm, Sanitary Connections	$50,000
Cost of Underground Parking	$600,000
Hard Construction Costs	$1,980,461
Landscaping	$92,258
Soft Costs	$258,347
Contingency on Hard and Soft Costs	$153,562
Residential DCC Charge	$26,263
Property Taxes	$44,108
Post Construction Holding Costs	$9,000
Interim Financing on Construction Costs	$102,974
Financing Fees/Costs	$48,766
Subtotal - Construction Costs	$3,455,914

Developer's Profit | $1,339,749

Profit Margin on Revenues/Value	20.7%
Profit Margin on Costs	26.2%

Notes:
Soft costs allow for permits, design, engineering, legal, survey, insurance, project management, consultants, warranties, deficiencies, misc.

Sample Developer's Proforma - All figures are Hypothetical for Illustrative Purposes Only
Townhouse Development

Major Assumptions (shading indicates figures that are inputs; unshaded cells are formulas)

Market (75%) and Affordable (25%) Townhouses

Revenue and Value
Average Sales Price Per Sq. Ft.	$750	per sq.ft. of net saleable residential space
Average Sales Price Per Sq. Ft. for Affordable Units	$525	per sq.ft. of net saleable affordable residential space

Site and Building Size
Site Size	0.28	acres or	12,301 sq. ft.
Site Frontage	32.07	meters	
Total Assumed Density	0.70	FAR	
Total Floorspace	8,611	sq.ft.	
Gross Residential Floorspace	8,611	sq.ft.	
Net Residential Floorspace	8,611	sq.ft.	
Average Gross Unit Size	1,435	sq.ft.	
Average Net Unit Size	1,435	sq.ft.	100.0% of gross area
Number of Units	6	units or	21 units per acre
Total Parking Stalls	9	stalls	1.5 stall per unit

Land Related Costs
Land Acquisition Cost	$1,179,566
Property Transfer Tax	$21,591
Financing Costs on Land Acquistion	$73,723

Construction Costs
On-Site Servicing (3)	$80,175	$2,500/m frontage
Water, Storm, Sanitary Connections (Includes water meter, if applicable)	$50,000	
Cost of Underground Parking	$450,000	$50,000 per spot
Hard Construction Costs	$230	per gross sq.ft.
Landscaping	$92,258	$15/sq ft for 50% of site area
Soft Costs	12.0%	of hard costs, servicing, landscaping
Contingency on Hard and Soft Costs	5.0%	of hard and soft costs
Residential DCC Charge	$0.00	Waived due to affordable housing units
Post Construction Holding Costs	$9,000.00	$500/unit for 50% of units for 6 months
Interim Financing on Construction Costs	5.0%	on 50% of hard and soft costs, assuming 1.25 year construction period
Financing Fees	1.50%	of hard and soft costs

Other Costs and Allowances
Rezoning Costs	$0	Prezoned land
Marketing on Residential	3.0%	of gross residential revenue
Sales Costs and Commissions	3.0%	of gross residential revenue
Residential Property Taxes	$40,800	0.683% of assessed value

Analysis

Revenue
Gross Multi-family Sales Revenue	$5,973,673
Less Marketing and Commissions	$358,420
Net Sales Revenue	$5,615,253

Land Related Costs
Land Acquisition Cost	$1,179,566
Property Transfer Tax	$21,591
Financing Costs on Land Acquistion	$73,723
Subtotal - Land and Related Costs	$1,274,880

Construction Costs
Rezoning Costs	$0	Prezoned land
On-Site Servicing (Upgrade of Adjacent Roads/Sidewalks/etc)	$80,175	
Water, Storm, Sanitary Connections	$50,000	
Cost of Underground Parking	$450,000	
Hard Construction Costs	$1,980,461	
Landscaping	$92,258	
Soft Costs	$258,347	
Contingency on Hard and Soft Costs	$145,562	
Residential DCC Charge	$0	Waived due to affordable housing units
Property Taxes	$40,800	
Post Construction Holding Costs	$9,000	
Interim Financing on Construction Costs	$96,800	
Financing Fees/Costs	$45,852	
Subtotal - Construction Costs	$3,249,255	

Developer's Profit	$1,091,117
Profit Margin on Revenues/Value	18.3%
Profit Margin on Costs	22.3%

Notes:
Soft costs allow for permits, design, engineering, legal, survey, insurance, project management, consultants, warranties, deficiencies, misc.

APPENDIX C | 145

Sample Developer's Proforma - All figures are Hypothetical for Illustrative Purposes Only
Market Apartment Development

Major Assumptions (shading indicates figures that are inputs; unshaded cells are formulas)

Market Apartments
Assumes 6 studio, 9-1BR, 5-2BR and 5-3BR units

Revenue and Value
Average Sales Price Per Sq. Ft.	$800	per sq.ft. of net saleable residential space
Average Sales Price Per Sq. Ft. for Affordable Units (not applicable)	$560	per sq.ft. of net saleable affordable residential space

Site and Building Size
Site Size	0.28	acres or	12,301 sq. ft.
Site Frontage	32.07	meters	
Total Assumed Density	1.50	FAR	
Total Floorspace	18,452	sq.ft.	
Gross Residential Floorspace	18,452	sq.ft.	
Net Residential Floorspace	15,684	sq.ft.	
Average Gross Unit Size	738	sq.ft.	
Average Net Unit Size	627	sq.ft.	85.0% of gross area
Number of Units	25	units or	89 units per acre
Total Parking Stalls	38	stalls	1.5 per unit

Land Related Costs
Land Acquisition Cost	$1,179,566
Property Transfer Tax	$21,591
Financing Costs on Land Acquistion	$73,723

Construction Costs
On-Site Servicing (3)	$80,175	$2,500/m frontage
Water, Storm, Sanitary Connections (Includes water meter, if applicable)	$75,000	
Cost of Underground Parking	$1,875,000	$50,000 per underground stall
Hard Construction Costs		$250 per gross sq.ft.
Landscaping	$92,258	$15/sq ft for 50% of site area
Soft Costs		12.0% of hard costs, servicing, landscaping
Contingency on Hard and Soft Costs		5.0% of hard and soft costs
Residential DCC Charge	$61,443	$3.33/per square foot
Post Construction Holding Costs	$37,500	$500/unit for 50% of units for 6 months
Interim Financing on Construction Costs		5.0% on 50% of hard and soft costs, assuming 1.50 year construction period
Financing Fees		1.50% of hard and soft costs

Other Costs and Allowances
Rezoning Costs	$10,000	
Marketing on Residential		3.0% of gross residential revenue
Sales Costs and Commissions		3.0% of gross residential revenue
Residential Property Taxes	$85,696	0.683% of assessed value

Analysis

Revenue
Gross Multi-family Sales Revenue	$12,547,020
Less Marketing and Commissions	$752,821
Net Sales Revenue	$11,794,199

Land Related Costs
Land Acquisition Cost	$1,179,566
Property Transfer Tax	$21,591
Financing Costs on Land Acquistion	$73,723
Subtotal - Land and Related Costs	$1,274,880

Construction Costs
Rezoning Costs	$10,000
On-Site Servicing (Upgrade of Adjacent Roads/Sidewalks/etc)	$80,175
Water, Storm, Sanitary Connections	$75,000
Cost of Underground Parking	$1,875,000
Hard Construction Costs	$4,612,875
Landscaping	$92,258
Soft Costs	$574,237
Contingency on Hard and Soft Costs	$365,977
Residential DCC Charge	$61,443
Property Taxes	$85,696
Post Construction Holding Costs	$37,500
Interim Financing on Construction Costs	$293,725
Financing Fees/Costs	$116,204
Subtotal - Construction Costs	$8,280,091

Developer's Profit	$2,239,228
Profit Margin on Revenues/Value	17.8%
Profit Margin on Costs	21.7%

Notes:
Soft costs allow for permits, design, engineering, legal, survey, insurance, project management, consultants, warranties, deficiencies, misc

Sample Developer's Proforma - All figures are Hypothetical for Illustrative Purposes Only
Market and Affordable Apartment Development

Major Assumptions (shading indicates figures that are inputs; unshaded cells are formulas)

75% Market Apartments and 25% Affordable
Assumes 6 studio, 9-1BR, 5-2BR and 5-3BR units - affordability by net area

Revenue and Value
Average Sales Price Per Sq. Ft.	$800	per sq.ft. of net saleable residential space
Average Sales Price Per Sq. Ft. for Affordable Units	$560	per sq.ft. of net saleable affordable residential space

Site and Building Size
Site Size	0.28	acres or	12,301 sq. ft.
Site Frontage	32.07	meters	
Total Assumed Density	1.50	FAR	
Total Floorspace	18,452	sq.ft.	
Gross Residential Floorspace	18,452	sq.ft.	
Net Residential Floorspace	15,684	sq.ft.	
Average Gross Unit Size	738	sq.ft.	
Average Net Unit Size	627	sq.ft.	85.0% of gross area
Number of Units	25	units or	89 units per acre
Total Parking Stalls	38	stalls	1.5 per unit

Land Related Costs
Land Acquisition Cost	$1,179,566
Property Transfer Tax	$21,591
Financing Costs on Land Acquistion	$73,723

Construction Costs
On-Site Servicing (3)	$80,175	$2,500/m frontage
Water, Storm, Sanitary Connections (Includes water meter, if applicable)	$75,000	
Cost of Underground Parking	$1,875,000	$50,000 per underground stall
Hard Construction Costs		$250 per gross sq.ft.
Landscaping	$92,258	$15/sq ft for 50% of site area
Soft Costs		12.0% of hard costs, servicing, landscaping
Contingency on Hard and Soft Costs		5.0% of hard and soft costs
Residential DCC Charge	$73,732.19	$3.33/per square foot
Post Construction Holding Costs	$37,500.00	$500/unit for 50% of units for 6 months
Interim Financing on Construction Costs		5.0% on 50% of hard and soft costs, assuming 1.50 year construction period
Financing Fees		1.50% of hard and soft costs

Other Costs and Allowances
Rezoning Costs	$10,000	
Marketing on Residential		3.0% of gross residential revenue
Sales Costs and Commissions		3.0% of gross residential revenue
Residential Property Taxes	$79,269	0.683% of assessed value

Analysis

Revenue
Gross Multi-family Sales Revenue	$11,605,994
Less Marketing and Commissions	$696,360
Net Sales Revenue	$10,909,634

Land Related Costs
Land Acquisition Cost	$1,179,566
Property Transfer Tax	$21,591
Financing Costs on Land Acquistion	$73,723
Subtotal - Land and Related Costs	$1,274,880

Construction Costs
Rezoning Costs	$10,000
On-Site Servicing (Upgrade of Adjacent Roads/Sidewalks/etc)	$80,175
Water, Storm, Sanitary Connections	$75,000
Cost of Underground Parking	$1,875,000
Hard Construction Costs	$4,612,875
Landscaping	$92,258
Soft Costs	$574,237
Contingency on Hard and Soft Costs	$365,977
Residential DCC Charge	$73,732
Property Taxes	$79,269
Post Construction Holding Costs	$37,500
Interim Financing on Construction Costs	$293,945
Financing Fees/Costs	$116,389
Subtotal - Construction Costs	$8,286,356

Developer's Profit
Developer's Profit	$1,348,397
Profit Margin on Revenues/Value	**11.6%**
Profit Margin on Costs	**13.1%**

Notes:
Soft costs allow for permits, design, engineering, legal, survey, insurance, project management, consultants, warranties, deficiencies, misc

Sample Developer's Proforma - All figures are Hypothetical for Illustrative Purposes Only
Market and Affordable Apartment Development

Major Assumptions (shading indicates figures that are inputs; unshaded cells are formulas)

75% Market Apartments and 25% Affordable
Assumes 3 studio, 7-1BR, 8-2BR and 8-3BR units - affordability by net area

Revenue and Value
Average Sales Price Per Sq. Ft.	$800	per sq.ft. of net saleable residential space
Average Sales Price Per Sq. Ft. for Affordable Units	$560	per sq.ft. of net saleable affordable residential space

Site and Building Size
Site Size	0.28	acres or	12,301 sq. ft.
Site Frontage	32.07	meters	
Total Assumed Density	1.80	FAR	
Total Floorspace	22,142	sq.ft.	
Gross Residential Floorspace	22,142	sq.ft.	
Net Residential Floorspace	18,821	sq.ft.	
Average Gross Unit Size	852	sq.ft.	
Average Net Unit Size	724	sq.ft.	85.0% of gross area
Number of Units	26	units or	92 units per acre
Total Parking Stalls	39	stalls	1.5 per unit

Land Related Costs
Land Acquisition Cost	$1,179,566
Property Transfer Tax	$21,591
Financing Costs on Land Acquistion	$73,723

Construction Costs
On-Site Servicing	$80,175	$2,500/m frontage
Water, Storm, Sanitary Connections (Includes water meter, if applicable)	$75,000	
Cost of Underground Parking	$1,950,000	$50,000 per underground stall
Hard Construction Costs	$250	per gross sq.ft.
Landscaping	$92,258	$15/sq ft for 50% of site area
Soft Costs	12.0%	of hard costs, servicing, landscaping
Contingency on Hard and Soft Costs	5.0%	of hard and soft costs
Residential DCC Charge	$73,732.19	Could be waived or reduced for affordable housing units
Post Construction Holding Costs	$39,000.00	$500/unit for 50% of units for 6 months
Interim Financing on Construction Costs	5.0%	on 50% of hard and soft costs, assuming 1.50 year construction period
Financing Fees	1.50%	of hard and soft costs

Other Costs and Allowances
Rezoning Costs	$10,000	
Marketing on Residential	3.0%	of gross residential revenue
Sales Costs and Commissions	3.0%	of gross residential revenue
Residential Property Taxes	$95,123	0.683% of assessed value

Analysis

Revenue
Gross Multi-family Sales Revenue	$13,927,192
Less Marketing and Commissions	$835,632
Net Sales Revenue	$13,091,561

Land Related Costs
Land Acquisition Cost	$1,179,566
Property Transfer Tax	$21,591
Financing Costs on Land Acquistion	$73,723
Subtotal - Land and Related Costs	$1,274,880

Construction Costs
Rezoning Costs	$10,000	
On-Site Servicing (Upgrade of Adjacent Roads/Sidewalks/etc)	$80,175	
Water, Storm, Sanitary Connections	$75,000	
Cost of Underground Parking	$1,950,000	
Hard Construction Costs	$5,535,450	
Landscaping	$92,258	
Soft Costs	$684,946	
Contingency on Hard and Soft Costs	$421,391	
Residential DCC Charge	$73,732	Could be waived or reduced for affordable housing units
Property Taxes	$95,123	
Post Construction Holding Costs	$39,000	
Interim Financing on Construction Costs	$338,178	
Financing Fees/Costs	$133,844	
Subtotal - Construction Costs	$9,529,097	

Developer's Profit
Developer's Profit	$2,287,584
Profit Margin on Revenues/Value	**16.4%**
Profit Margin on Costs	**19.7%**

Notes:
Soft costs allow for permits, design, engineering, legal, survey, insurance, project management, consultants, warranties, deficiencies, misc.

GLOSSARY

Adolescent: All persons between the ages of 10 and 19, as defined by the United Nations. As children up to the age of 18, most adolescents are protected under the Convention on the Rights of the Child. Yet, they have distinct needs and vulnerabilities and are, therefore, often identified as a distinct group.

Adult: All persons 18 years of age and older, as defined by the United Nations.

Affordable Housing: Defined as housing which has a mortgage payment or rent that does not exceed 30% of income for low to moderate income households having an income that is 80% or less than the median household income for the community, and may include low income subsidized housing administered by the municipality, BC Housing, Capital Region Housing, or other non-profit housing societies in the region.

Apartment: A residential use where a building or buildings with interior access on a single lot are used for three or more self-contained rental dwelling units.

"As-of-right" Development: The right to develop a property in any manner, provided the proposed development complies with all zoning regulations.

Caregiver: A related or unrelated person who is actively engaged in providing care to a child, including parents, grandparents, nannies, baby sitters, foster parents, and/or other paid or unpaid persons providing child care.

Child/Children: All persons being below the age of eighteen years, in accordance with the United Nations Convention on the Rights of the Child.

Co-housing: An intentional community of private dwellings clustered around shared space. Co-housing communities define their collective approach to aging in community, including the limits of co-care that they are willing to provide for one another.

Complete Community: A complete community has a balance and mix of residential and employment uses, a range of housing types and tenures, a distribution of public services, and a range of transportation services.

Co-operative Housing: A co-operative is an autonomous association of persons united voluntarily to meet their common economic, social, and cultural needs through a democratically-controlled housing development. Members typically own a share of the co-op, but not the individual unit they live in.

Core Housing Need: Core housing need is a measure of housing need in Canada. Core housing need reports on the number of households in a community who are unable to find housing that is suitable in size, in good repair and affordable without spending 30 per cent or more of their income on housing.

Density Bonuses: Regulatory measures that permit developers to build at higher densities than current zoning allows in exchange for community amenity contributions such as affordable housing.

Detached Accessory Dwelling Unit: An additional, self-contained rental dwelling unit, which is secondary to a principal dwelling unit and is located on the same legal lot as the principal dwelling unit with which it is associated.

Development Permit Area: Areas that have been designated under the Local Government Act as requiring issuance of a development permit prior to the commencement of development.

Duplex: A building which contains two principal dwelling units attached to each other, either side by side, back to front, or above and below, and the two units together have open space on all sides.

Early Childhood: A child aged 0-4 years.

Family: Family refers to households that include children under 19 years of age. These children may live with a parent, a grandparent, foster parent, or a caregiver.

Family Housing: Independent housing for households with a minimum of two people, including at least one dependent child.

Fourplex: A building that contains four principal dwelling units attached to each other, and the four units together have open space on all sides.

Full Spectrum CPTED: Full Spectrum Crime Prevention Through Environmental Design (CPTED) combines placemaking, restorative practices, compassionate enquiry, arts for social change, and peace building methodologies to address community safety, reduce crime, embrace culture, and support social connection.

Ground-Oriented Housing: Ground-oriented housing refers to single detached or multi-unit housing that is oriented toward or has direct access from the ground.

Housing Action Plans: A Housing Action Plan (HAP) establishes a framework that municipalities can use to identify objectives and actions for increasing the supply, diversity, and affordability of housing in a municipality. This tool can be used to raise the profile of housing issues in the community, to implement housing policies and practices to help address housing affordability and supply, help target those policies to local needs, and assess the effectiveness of municipal actions in meeting housing needs.

Housing Agreements: Housing agreements are a regulatory tool that takes the form of contractual arrangements between local governments and property owners or housing providers that govern the tenure, occupancy, rent levels and resale restrictions of affordable housing units. When in place, these agreements may help ensure the long-term affordability of housing units.

Housing Continuum: The housing continuum provides an important organizing framework for understanding housing needs and housing choices. In most cases the housing continuum can include emergency shelters, transitional/supportive housing, non-market housing, market rental housing, and ownership housing.

Housing Tenure: refers to the financial arrangements under which someone has the right to live in a house or apartment. The most common forms are tenancy, in which rent is paid to a landlord, and owner-occupancy.

Inclusionary Zoning Policies: Inclusionary zoning policies require the provision of some type of affordable housing as part of rezoning for a development. These voluntary policies may dictate that a percentage of units or square footage, or a specific number of units be affordable. Some policies require units to be built on site, others allow for units to be transferred to other sites, and some permit cash-in lieu contributions.

Infill Housing: Refers to the insertion of additional housing units into an existing neighbourhood. Infill housing can be provided as additional units built on the same lot, by dividing existing homes into multiple units, or by subdividing existing lots. Many municipalities have established guidelines for infill housing.

Mixed-use Development: A pedestrian-friendly development that blends residential, commercial, cultural, institutional, or entertainment uses.

Multi-family Dwelling: A residential building that contains three or more dwelling units, and includes triplex, fourplex, townhouse, row houses, and apartment forms.

Non-Market Housing: Government assisted housing which was built through one of a number of government funded programs. This housing is typically managed by the non-profit or co-op housing sectors. Most non-market housing receives an operating subsidy. (See also non-profit housing, social housing, and co-operative housing).

Non-Profit Housing: Non-profit housing is housing that is owned and operated by non-profit housing providers. This housing is typically built through government funded housing supply programs.

Open Space: Refers to "open to the sky" areas identified as forests, woods, wetlands, lawns, front and back yards, landscaped areas, courtyards, pathways, and playing fields.

Preschooler: A child aged 3-5 years.

Private Market Rental Housing: The private rental market provides the majority of low cost housing. This can include purpose-built rental housing as well as housing supplied through the secondary rental market, including basement apartments and rented condominiums.

Row House: Side-by-side units, separated by party walls, each with direct access from grade and access to private outdoor space. The owners of row houses own not only the unit, but also the land below it. As a result, each unit requires a separate water and sewer hook-up.

Secondary Suite: An accessory, self-contained dwelling unit with cooking facilities, located in a single-detached home.

School-Age: Refers to children between the ages of 5 and 12.

Senior: Refers to a person who is aged 65 or older.

Single Detached Dwelling: A residential dwelling not attached to any other dwelling or structure (except its own garage, shed, or secondary suite). A single family detached dwelling has open space on all sides and has no dwellings either above it or below it (except, in some cases, a secondary suite).

Social Housing: Social housing refers to housing built under Federal, Federal/Provincial or Provincial housing programs and is designed to accommodate households with low to moderate incomes in core housing need. Social housing includes public housing as well as non-profit and co-op housing.

Toddler: A child aged 12-36 months (1-3 years).

Townhouse: A single building that is comprised of three or more dwelling units that are separated from one another by party walls extending from foundation to roof. Each dwelling unit has a separate and direct entrance from grade. The owners of townhouses own their dwelling unit and the townhouse development is built on shared property. As a result, only one sewer and water hook-up may be required for the entire development.

Triplex: A building which contains three principal dwelling units attached to each other, and the three units together have open space on all sides.

Universal Design: refers to broad-spectrum ideas meant to produce buildings, products, and environments that are inherently accessible to everyone, including older people, people with disabilities, and people without disabilities.

Young Adult: All persons between the ages of 15 and 24 years, as defined by the United Nations.

Youth: All persons between the ages of 16 and 19 years, as defined by the BC Child, Family and Community Service Act.

BOOKS

Beasley, Larry. Vancouverism. Vancouver: UBC Press, 2019.

Bishop, Kate and Linda Corkery, eds. Designing Cities with Children and Young People: Beyond Playgrounds and Skate Parks. New York: Routledge, 2017.

Derr, Victoria, Lousie Chawla, and Mara Mintzer. Placemaking with Children and Youth: Participatory Practices for Planning Sustainable Communities. New York: New Village Press, 2018.

Friedman, Avi. Neighbourhood: Designing a Liveable Community. Montréal: Véhicule Press, 2018.

Gravel, Ryan. Where We Want to Live: Reclaiming Infrastructure for a New Generation of Cities. New York: St. Martin's Press, 2016.

Greenberg, Ken. Walking Home: The Life and Lessons of a City Builder. Toronto: Random House Canada, 2011.

Hallsmith, Gwendolyn. The Key to Sustainable Cities: Meeting Human Needs Transforming Community Systems. Gabriola Island: New Society Publishers, 2003.

Harcourt, Mike, Ken Cameron, and Sean Rossiter. City Making in Paradise: Nine Decisions that Saved Vancouver. Vancouver: Douglas & McIntyre Ltd., 2007.

Kellner, Jessica. Housing Reclaimed: Sustainable Homes for Next to Nothing. Gabriola Island: New Society Publishers, 2011.

Lange, Alexandra. The Design of Childhood: How the Material World Shaped Independent Kids. New York: Bloomsbury Publishing Inc., 2018.

Lorinc, John. The New City: How the Crisis in Canada's Urban Centres is Reshaping the Nation. Toronto: Penguin Canada, 2006.

McKnight, John and Peter Block. The Abundant Community: Awakening the Power of Families and Neighborhoods. Oakland: Berrett-Koehler Publishers, Inc., 2012.

Montgomery, Charles. Happy City: Transforming Our Lives Through Urban Design. Doubleday Canada, 2013.

BIBLIOGRAPHY

Register, Richard. Ecocities: Rebuilding Cities in Balance with Nature, Revised ed. Gabriola Island: New Society Publishers, 2006.

Rose, Johnathan F.P. The Well-Tempered City: What Modern Science, Ancient Civilizations, and Human Nature Teach Us About the Future of Urban Life. New York: Harper Wave, 2016.

Roy, Kishone. Make Housing Central: British Columbia and the Affordable Housing Crisis. Vancouver: Indyhan Books, 2017. Kindle edition.

Stein, Samuel. Capital City: Gentrification and the Real Estate State. London: Verso, 2019.

Studer, Diana. Put Play to Work: Engaging Children in the Design Process through Play-Based Charrettes. RAIC 690 A&B Syllabus Diploma Project. Victoria, 2018.

Westley, Frances, Brenda Zimmerman, and Michael Quinn Patton. Getting to Maybe. Random House Canada, 2006.

VIDEOS AND NEW MEDIA

Mintzer, Mara. "How Kids Can Help Design Cities." Filmed November 2017. TEDxMileHigh, 14:25. Accessed May 7, 2019. https://www.ted.com/talks/mara_mintzer_how_kids_can_help_design_cities?language=en

Thomas, Ren. "How to plan for affordable housing". Canadian Institute of Planners. Filmed June 5, 2019. YouTube video, 1:25:52. Posted June 6, 2019. https://www.youtube.com/watch?v=Env0nNFOwI8&feature=youtu.be (check citation!)

ONLINE PUBLICATIONS

880 Cities, Bernard Van Leer Foundation, and Urban 95. 2017. "Building Better Cities with Young Children and Families." bernardvanleer.org https://bernardvanleer.org/app/uploads/2017/10/BvLF-8-80-Cities-Report-Final.pdf (accessed May 12, 2019)

Alexander, Christopher, Sara Ishikawa, and Murray Silverstein. A Pattern Language: Towns, Buildings, Construction. Oxford University Press: New York, 1977.

Altus Group. 2018 Canadian Cost Guide. http://creston.ca/DocumentCenter/View/1957/

Altus-2018-Construction-Cost-Guide-web-1 (accessed October 11, 2019)

ARUP. Cities Alive: Designing for Urban Childhoods. London: ARUP, 2017. https://www.arup.com/perspectives/publications/research/section/cities-alive-designing-for-urban-childhoods (accessed June 26, 2019).

BC Rental Housing Coalition. "An Affordable Housing Plan for BC." Housing Central. [No date]. https://housingcentral.ca/SITES/HousingCentral/Affordable_Housing_Plan/HousingCentral/Affordable_Rental_Housing_Plan.aspx?hkey=433f9af0-e946-4a37-b827-94f68667dc0b (accessed September 24, 2019)

Bernard van Leer Foundation. Compendium of Best Practices of Child-Friendly Cities. National Institute of Urban Affairs: New Delhi, April 2017. https://bernardvanleer.org/app/uploads/2017/10/Compendium_of_Best_Practices_of_Child_Friendly_Cities_2017.pdf (accessed August 5, 2019).

Bernard van Leer Foundation. "Urban95." bernardvanleer.org https://bernardvanleer.org/solutions/urban95/ (accessed May 14, 2019)

Canada Mortgage and Housing Corporation. "Housing Standards." Housing in Canada Online. https://cmhc.beyond2020.com/HiCODefinitions_EN.html#_Suitable_dwellings (accessed June 21, 2019)

Cheung, Christopher. "The Key to a Family-Friendly City? Family-Sized Housing." The Tyee, November 25, 2016. https://thetyee.ca/News/2016/11/25/Family-Friendly-Housing/ (accessed August 3, 2019).

Child, Family and Community Service Act, RSBC. 1996, c-46. http://www.bclaws.ca/civix/document/id/complete/statreg/96046_01#section1 (accessed October 23, 2019).

City of Belfast. A Plan Fit for Children: Health at the Heart of the Local Development Plan, June 2017. https://www.belfasthealthycities.com/sites/default/files/publications/A%20Plan%20Fit%20for%20Children.pdf (accessed September 1, 2019)

City of Kingston. 2018 Vacancy Rate Implications: Report Number 19-065. Information Report to Council, March 5, 2019. https://www.cityofkingston.ca/documents/10180/32824678/City-Council_Meeting-10-2019_Report-19-065_2018-Vacancy-Rate-Implications.pdf/49d393d4-99b3-416b-8580-526268028ad2 (accessed August 1, 2019).

City of Portland. Principles of Child Friendly Housing, July 2007. http://www.courtyardhousing.org/downloads/ChildFriendlyHousing.pdf (accessed May 14, 2019)

City of Toronto. 2017.Growing Up: Planning for Children in New Vertical Communities

Draft Urban Design Guidelines, May 2017. https://www.toronto.ca/legdocs/mmis/2017/pg/bgrd/backgroundfile-103920.pdf (accessed October 17, 2019).

City of Vancouver. 2018. Criteria Established For Interim Rezoning Policy for Affordable Housing Choices, June 2018. https://vancouver.ca/files/cov/Affordable-housing-choices-interim-rezoning-policy.pdf (accessed May 1, 2019).

City of Vancouver. Housing Design and Technical Guidelines, January 22, 2018. Version 9.7. https://vancouver.ca/files/cov/housing-design-and-technical-guidelines.pdf (accessed May 1, 2019).

City of Vancouver. High Density Housing for Families with Children Guidelines. July 13, 2016. https://vancouver.ca/files/cov/family-room-housing-mix-policy-for-rezoning-projects-2016-07-13.pdf (accessed October 3, 2019).

City of Vancouver. Family Room: Housing Mix Policy for Rezoning Projects . March 24, 1992. https://guidelines.vancouver.ca/H004.pdf (accessed October 1, 2019).

Coley, Rebekah Levine, Tama Leventhal, Alicia Doyle Lynch, and Melissa Kull. "Relations between Housing Characteristics and the Well-Being of Low-Income Children and Adolescents." Developmental Psychology, September 2013; 49(9): 1775–1789. doi:10.1037/a0031033.

Community Charter, SBC. 2003, c-26. http://www.bclaws.ca/civix/document/id/complete/statreg/03026_07#section226 (accessed October 4, 2019).

Coriolis Consulting Corp. Financial Analysis of Urban Development Opportunities in the Fairfield and Gonzales Communities, Victoria BC. Report prepared for the City of Victoria. December 5, 2016. https://www.victoria.ca/assets/Departments/Planning~Development/Community~Planning/Local~Area~Planning/Fairfield~Gonzales/Fairfield/Financial%20analysis%20for%20urban%20residential%20-%202Dec2016%20-%20Copy.pdf (accessed September 3, 2019).

Corporation of the District of Saanich. Zoning Bylaw 8200. September 2003. https://www.saanich.ca/assets/Local~Government/Documents/Planning/zone8200.pdf (accessed

September 29, 2019)

Cox, Daniel and Ryan Streeter. "Having a Library or Cafe Down the Block Could Change Your Life." City Lab, May 20, 2019. https://www.citylab.com/life/2019/05/having-library-or-cafe-down-block-could-change-your-life/589813/ (accessed June 27, 2019).

CMHC. "Socio-Economic Inequalities in Housing Issues: Measurement and Beyond." Non-Technical Research Summary. June 2019. https://www.cmhc-schl.gc.ca/en/data-and-research/publications-and-reports/research-insight-socioeconomic-inequalities-housing-issues-measurement-beyond (accessed August 6, 2019).

Crook, Adrian. "How to Rent a Family Friendly Condo." 5 Kids 1 Condo (blog), July 2, 2015. http://5kids1condo.com/how-to-rent-a-family-friendly-condo/ (accessed July 9, 2019).

Crook, Adrian. "Square-Foot Hours: Designing 24-Hour Spaces." 5 Kids 1 Condo (blog), January 26, 2016. http://5kids1condo.com/square-foot-hours-designing-24-hour-spaces/ (accessed July 9, 2019).

Danenberg, Rosa, Vivian Doumpa, and Hans Karssenberg, eds. The City at Eye Level for Kids. Rotterdam: STIPO Publishing, 2018. www.thecityateyelevel.com (accessed June 14, 2019).

Derbyshire, David. "How Children Lost the Right to Roam in Four Generations." Daily Mail, June 15, 2007. https://www.dailymail.co.uk/news/article-462091/How-children-lost-right-roam-generations.html (accessed October 20, 2019).

Dietz, Robert D. "The Social Consequences of Homeownership." Report. Homeownership Alliance. June 18, 2003. http://www.bluefence.com/files/social_consequences_study.pdf (accessed July 9, 2019).

Dunn, James R.. "Levels of Influence in the Built Environment on the Promotion of Healthy Child Development." Healthcare Quarterly, 15 Special Issue(4) July 2012: 32-37. doi:10.12927/hcq.2013.22944 (accessed October 25, 2019).

Derr, Victoria, Louise Chawla, Mara Mintzer, Debra Flanders Cushing, and Willem Van Vliet. "A City for All Citizens: Integrating Children and Youth from Marginalized Populations into City Planning." Buildings. 3, 482-505 (July 2013); doi:10.3390/buildings3030482 (accessed September 2, 2019)

Edwards, C.P., Knoche, L., and Kumru, A.. "Play Patterns and Gender." Encyclopedia of Women and Gender, vol. 2. Ed. Judith Worrell (San Diego: Academic Press, 2001): 814.

https://digitalcommons.unl.edu/cgi/viewcontent.cgi?article=1610&context=psychfacpub (accessed August 2, 2019)

Fowler, Patrick J., and Anne F. Farrell. "Housing and Child Well Being: Implications for Research, Policy, and Practice." Am J Community Psychology, September 2017; 60(1-2): 3–8. doi: 10.1002/ajcp.12154 (accessed August 14, 2019).

Gill, Tim. "How to build cities fit for children." Rethinking childhood (blog), April 30, 2019. https://rethinkingchildhood.com/2019/04/30/building-cities-fit-for-children_churchill-fellowship-child-friendly-urban-planning-design/ (accessed August 1, 2019).

Government of Canada. A Place to Call Home: Canada's National Housing Strategy. 2017. https://www.placetocallhome.ca/-/media/sf/project/placetocallhome/pdfs/canada-national-housing-strategy.pdf (accessed August 6, 2019).

Hyndman, Brendon. "Let them play! Kids need freedom from play restrictions to develop." The Conversation, May 23, 2019. https://theconversation.com/let-them-play-kids-need-freedom-from-play-restrictions-to-develop-117586 (accessed June 25, 2019).

Karsten, Lia. "Children's Use of Public Space: The Gendered World of the Playground" Childhood 10, iss. 4 (2003): 466. http://journals.sagepub.com/doi/abs/10.1177/0907568203104005 (accessed August 10, 2019)

Karsten, Lia, "From a top-down to a bottom-up urban discourse: (re)constructing the city in a family-inclusive way." Journal of Housing and the Built Environment April 30, 2009. 24:317–329 DOI 10.1007/s10901-009-9145-1 (accessed June 7, 2019)

Kirk, Mimi." Drawing Up an Urban Planning Manual for Chicago Teens." CityLab, April 5, 2017. https://www.citylab.com/life/2017/04/chicago-architecture-foundation-no-small-plans-graphic-novel-teens/521802/ (accessed October 2, 2019).

Land Title Act, RSBC. 1996, c-250. http://www.bclaws.ca/civix/document/id/complete/statreg/96250_00 (accessed October 3, 2019).

Lange, Alexandra. "The Moms Aren't Wrong: Why Planning for Children Would Make Cities Better for All." Alexandra Lange (blog), February 1, 2011. https://www.alexandralange.net/articles/12/the-moms-aren-t-wrong-why-planning-for-children-would-make-cities-better-for-all (accessed October 22, 2019).

Lárusdóttir A. R. and Dederichs, A. "Evacuation Dynamics of Children: Walking Speeds, Flow

Through Doors in Daycare Centres." Ph.D. Research, Technical University of Denmark, 2016, http://www.kias.org.uk/wp-content/uploads/2016/02/Walking-speed-children.pdf (accessed September 2, 2019).

Lemmon, Wayne. 2007. "Pro-Forma 101: Part 1 – Getting Familiar With a Basic Tool of Real Estate Analysis." Planners Web, December 23, 2013. http://plannersweb.com/2013/12/proforma-101-getting-familiar-with-a-basic-tool-of-real-estate-analysis/ (accessed October 2, 2019).

Lin, Ying-Tzu. "Child-friendly Cities from an Urban Planner's Perspective." in The City at Eye Level for Kids, edited by Danenberg, Rosa, Vivian Doumpa, and Hans Karssenberg, p.42. Rotterdam: STIPO Publishing, 2018. https://thecityateyelevel.com/app/uploads/2019/06/eBook_CAEL_Kids_Book_Design_Kidsgecomprimeerd.pdf (accessed June 14, 2019).

Local Government Act, RSBC. 2015, c-1. http://www.bclaws.ca/civix/document/id/complete/statreg/r15001_00 (accessed October 3, 2019).

LoIacono, Marni, Carolyn Rodgers, Ellen Silver, Jamie Sclafane, and Laurie Bauman. "Engaging and sustaining adolescents in community-based participatory research: structuring a youth-friendly community-based participatory research environment." Family and Community Health. 2015;38(1):22–32. doi:10.1097/FCH.0000000000000057 (accessed June 3, 2019).

McAllister, Catherine. "Child Friendly Cities and Land Use Planning: Implications for children's health." Environments Journal. Vol 35 (3): 2008. http://citeseerx.ist.psu.edu/viewdoc/download?doi=10.1.1.393.63&rep=rep1&type=pdf (Accessed November 4, 2019).

Metro Vancouver Regional Housing. 2012 What Works: Affordable Housing Initiatives in Metro Vancouver Municipalities. Report. November 2012. http://www.metrovancouver.org/services/regional-planning/PlanningPublications/1267_WhatWorks_LR.pdf (accessed August 3, 2019).

Mortensen, Michael. "Making Apartments Work Harder: the 3rd Bedroom Challenge." Plan the Liveable City (blog), January 19, 2016. https://michaelmortensenblog.com/2016/01/19/making-apartments-work-harder-the-3rd-bedroom-challenge/ (accessed June 27, 2019).

Newitz, Annalee. "Want your kids to be better off than you? Move to a high-density city." Ars Technica, February 2, 2016. https://arstechnica.com/science/2016/02/want-your-kids-to-be-better-off-than-you-move-to-a-high-density-city/?utm_content=bufferd8fdb&utm_

medium=social&utm_source=twitter.com&utm_campaign=buffer (accessed July 9, 2019).

O'Sullivan, Feargus. "Rebuilding a City from the Eye of a Child." City Lab, December 17, 2018. https://www.citylab.com/equity/2018/12/kid-friendly-policy-tirana-urban-planning/578164/ (accessed June 27, 2019).

Patuszyñska, Beata. "Barriers for Warsaw's Youngest Citizens on their Way to School." in The City at Eye Level for Kids, edited by Danenberg, Rosa, Vivian Doumpa, and Hans Karssenberg, p.247. Rotterdam: STIPO Publishing, 2018. https://thecityateyelevel.com/app/uploads/2019/06/eBook_CAEL_Kids_Book_Design_Kidsgecomprimeerd.pdf (accessed June 14, 2019).

Peñalosa, Enrique. "The Politics of Happiness." Yes!, May 20, 2004. https://www.yesmagazine.org/issues/finding-courage/the-politics-of-happiness (accessed September 25, 2019).

Province of British Columbia. Land Use Agreements Between Local Governments & Landowners. https://www.placetocallhome.ca/-/media/sf/project/placetocallhome/pdfs/canada-national-housing-strategy.pdf (accessed September 6, 2019).

Province of British Columbia. Residential Rental Tenure Zoning – Bulletin https://www2.gov.bc.ca/assets/gov/british-columbians-our-governments/local-governments/planning-land-use/residential_rental_zoning_bulletin1.pdf Ministry of Municipal Affairs and Housing, July 3, 2018. (accessed July 2, 2019).

Ratcliffe, Caroline. "Child Poverty and Adult Success." Urban Institute, September 2015. https://www.urban.org/sites/default/files/publication/65766/2000369-Child-Poverty-and-Adult-Success.pdf (accessed August 2, 2019).

Reardon, Mitchell. "Is Vancouver Ready to Grow from Laneways to Living Lanes?" Spacing Vancouver, October 3, 2016. http://spacing.ca/vancouver/2016/10/03/vancouver-ready-grow-laneways-living-lanes/ (accessed October 21, 2019).

Shier, Harry. "Pathways to Participation: Openings, Opportunities and Obligations." Children & Society 15(2):107-117 (March 2001). doi: 10.1002/chi.617 (accessed November 1, 2019).

Stanford Children's Health. "The Growing Child: School-Age." Lucille Packard Children's Hospital Stanford. https://www.stanfordchildrens.org/en/topic/default?id=the-growing-child-school-age-6-to-12-years-90-P02278 (accessed September 1, 2019).

State of New South Wales. "Low Rise Medium Density Design Guide for Complying

Development." State of NSW, Department of Planning and Environment, 2017. https://www.planning.nsw.gov.au/-/media/Files/DPE/Manuals-and-guides/Low-rise-medium-density-design-guide-for-complying-development-2018-07-24.pdf (accessed October 22, 2019).

Statistics Canada. 2019. Housing suitability of private household. Ottawa. Released January 21.2013. Last modified 2019-04-03. www23.statcan.gc.ca/imdb/p3Var.pl?Function=DEC&Id=100731 (accessed September 17, 2019)

Statistics Canada. 2017. British Columbia [Province] and Canada [Country] (table). Census Profile. 2016 Census. Statistics Canada Catalogue no. 98-316-X2016001. Ottawa. Released November 29, 2017. https://www12.statcan.gc.ca/census-recensement/2016/dp-pd/prof/index.cfm?Lang=E (accessed September 26, 2019).

Tetloff, Meredith & Griffith, Matt. "Engaging Adolescents as Community Organizers." Journal of Youth Development. 3. 89-95. (November 2016). 10.5195/JYD.2008.309. (accessed Octover 3, 2019)

United Nations Children's Fund (UNICEF). "Adolescent Demographics." April 2016. https://data.unicef.org/topic/adolescents/overview/ (accessed September 20, 2019).

United Nations Children's Fund (UNICEF). Building a World Fit for Children. . New York: UNICEF, Division of Communication, April 2003. https://www.unicef.org/publications/files/pub_build_wffc_en.pdf (accessed June 2, 2019).

United Nations Children's Fund (UNICEF). Shaping Urbanization for Children: A Handbook on Child-Responsive Urban Planning. New York: UNICEF, Division of Data, Research, and Policy, 2018. https://www.unicef.org/publications/files/UNICEF_Shaping_urbanization_for_children_handbook_2018.pdf (accessed June 2, 2019).

United Nations Department of Economic and Social Affairs (UN DESA). "68% of the world population projected to live in urban areas by 2050." May 16, 2018. New York: UN DESA. https://www.un.org/development/desa/en/news/population/2018-revision-of-world-urbanization-prospects.html (accessed June 23, 2019).

United Nations Office of the High Commissioner. Convention on the Rights of the Child. Resolution of the General Assembly. November 20, 1989. https://www.ohchr.org/en/professionalinterest/pages/crc.aspx (accessed July 4, 2019).

University of Idaho. 2004. "Housing." Lecture notes. https://www.webpages.uidaho.edu/

larc301/lectures/housing.htm (accessed October 1, 2019)

University of Iowa. "Why children struggle to cross busy streets safely: New research shows perceptual judgment, motor skills not fully developed until age 14." ScienceDaily, April 20, 2017. https://www.sciencedaily.com/releases/2017/04/170420090208.htm (accessed July 11, 2019).

Urban Land Institute. Bending the Cost Curve: Solutions to Expand the Supply of Affordable Rentals. Washington: Urban Land Institute, Terwilliger Center for Housing, 2014. http://uli.org/wp-content/uploads/ULI-Documents/BendingCostCurve-Solutions_2014_web.pdf (accessed May 28, 2019).

Van den Berg, Marguerite. "City Children and Genderfied Neighbourhoods: The New Generation as Urban Regeneration Strategy." International Journal of Urban and Regional Research, Vol 37.2 (March 2013), pp 523-36. doi: 10.1111/j.1468-2427.2012.01172.x

Wegmann, Jake. "Is there room for children in booming western cities? Empirical evidence from Austin, Denver, and Portland.," Cities, Vol 96 (January 2020). DOI: https://doi.org/10.1016/j.cities.2019.102403

Whitzman, Carolyn. (2017). Creating Child-Friendly Living Environments in Central Cities: Vertical Living Kids. doi: 10.1007/978-981-287-035-3_6

World Health Organization. "Checklist of Essential Features of Age-friendly Cities." 2007. Accessed October 4, 2019. https://www.who.int/ageing/publications/Age_friendly_cities_checklist.pdf

World Health Organization. Global Age-friendly Cities: A Guide. France: WHO Press, 2007. Accessed September 28, 2019. https://www.who.int/ageing/publications/Global_age_friendly_cities_Guide_English.pdf

PRINT JOURNALS

Coughlan, Anne T., Hallie Preskill, and Tessie Tzavaras Catsambas. "An Overview of Appreciative Inquiry in Evaluation," New Directions for Evaluation: Using Appreciative Inquiry in Evaluation, no. 100 (Winter 2003): 5-22.

Hanson Smart, Dawn and Mariann Mann. "Incorporating Appriciative Inquiry Methods to Evaluate a Youth Development Program," New Directions for Evaluation: Using

Appreciative Inquiry in Evaluation, no. 100 (Winter 2003): 63-74.

Quinn Patton, Michael. "Inquiry into Appreciative Evaluation," New Directions for Evaluation: Using Appreciative Inquiry in Evaluation, no. 100 (Winter 2003): 85-98.

Rogers, Patricia J. and Dugan Fraser. "Appreciating Appreciative Inquiry," New Directions for Evaluation: Using Appreciative Inquiry in Evaluation, no. 100 (Winter 2003): 75-83.

PAGE	IMAGE SOURCE
iv	Kundu, Senjuti. *Girl with Paint of Body*. [Photograph] (2017). Image used under license from Unsplash. https://unsplash.com/photos/JfolIjRnveY
1	Sofia Agnello, 2019.
2	Kristin Agnello, 2019.
6	Blum, Brina. [Untitled Photograph] (2018). Image used under license from Unsplash. https://unsplash.com/photos/d-RwmHvHPPg
7	Kristin Agnello, 2019
9	Lilia Agnello, 2019.
10	De Silva, Sai.. [Untitled Photograph] (2015). Image used under license from Unsplash. https://unsplash.com/photos/E68j7MQ4u3Q
61	Sofia Agnello, 2019
62	Kristin Agnello, 2019
65	Agnello, K. (2017). "Can you Make the Light?" Originally published in "Strollers and Scooters: Perspectives of a Millennial Planner Living in a Retirement Community." Plan Canada, vol. 57, iss. 3, 26-28.
73	Wiedemann, Ken. *Portland Maine Rooftops stock photo*. [Photograph] (2010). Image used under license from iStock. https://www.istockphoto.com/ca/photo/portland-maine-rooftops-gm171149865-14674116
74	Babakin, Roman. Apartment residential house facade architecture with kid playground sun light. [Photograph] (2019). Image used under license from iStock. https://www.istockphoto.com/ca/photo/apartment-residential-house-facade-architecture-with-kid-playground-sun-light-gm1087216880-291691429
75	Lordn. Preschool teacher with children playing with didactic toys. [Photograph] (2018). Image used under license from iStock. https://www.istockphoto.com/ca/photo/preschool-teacher-with-children-playing-with-didactic-toys-gm1044044044-279447453
76	Babakin, Roman. Fragment in Modern residential flat apartment building exterior. [Photograph] (2019). Image used under license from iStock. https://www.istockphoto.com/ca/photo/fragment-in-modern-residential-flat-apartment-building-exterior-gm1185257113-333959857
77	Geber86. Happy Family. [Photograph] (2016). Image used under license from iStock. https://www.istockphoto.com/ca/photo/happy-family-gm528552736-93020767

IMAGE CREDITS

78	Bialasiewicz, Katarzyna. Multifunctional bedroom and workspace interior with bed and desk.. [Photograph] (2019). https://www.istockphoto.com/ca/photo/multifunctional-bedroom-and-workspace-interior-with-bed-and-desk-gm1168256209-322504231
79	Bialasiewicz, Katarzyna. Clever solutions for a tiny apartment. [Photograph] (2016). https://www.istockphoto.com/ca/photo/clever-solutions-for-a-tiny-apartment-gm612753404-105641367
80	Chuttersnap. Motorcycles in warehouse hall. [Photograph] (2017). Image used under license from Unsplash. https://unsplash.com/photos/LJsCWMVDKMk
81	monkeybusinessimages. Excited Children Arriving Home With Parents. [Photograph] (2017). https://www.istockphoto.com/ca/photo/excited-children-arriving-home-with-parents-gm670900812-122741129
82	Sikkema, Kelly. Waking up to check for snow, with the inevitable "Is school cancelled today?!" [Photograph] (2018). Image used under license from Unsplash. https://unsplash.com/photos/4l2Ml8-MLUg
83	vchal. Sunlite light tube system for transporting natural daylight from roof into room. [3D rendered illustration] (2018). Image used under license from iStock. https://www.istockphoto.com/ca/photo/sunlite-light-tube-system-for-transporting-natural-daylight-from-roof-into-room-3d-gm935317736-255950405
84	Briscoe, Jason. [Untitled Photograph] (2016). Image used under license from Unsplash. https://unsplash.com/photos/Eu4_4e8_ltE
85	Borba, Jonathan. [Untitled Photograph] (2019). Image used under license from Unsplash. https://unsplash.com/photos/JzCC_b280fM
86	rawpixel. Family planting vegetable from backyard garden. [Photograph] (2017). Image used under license from iStock. https://www.istockphoto.com/ca/photo/family-planting-vegetable-from-backyard-garden-gm671270794-122842581
87	Babakin, Roman. Children playground at Modern residential apartment house complex outdoor facility. [Photograph] (2019). Image used under license from iStock. https://www.istockphoto.com/ca/photo/children-playground-at-modern-residential-apartment-house-complex-outdoor-facility-gm1146069046-308696139
89	Kyrylyuk, Volodymyr. Apartment Buildings. [Photograph] (2017). Image used under license from iStock. https://www.istockphoto.com/ca/photo/apartment-buildings-gm645199404-116940071
90	Elenathewise. Modern Townhouses. [Photograph] (2011). Image used under license from iStock. https://www.istockphoto.com/ca/photo/modern-townhouses-gm134987449-18406664
91	Wallis, Marcus. Two children sitting on ground with dried leaves. [Photograph] (2018). Image used under license from Unsplash. https://unsplash.com/photos/MTeZ5FmCGCU
92	Ridofranz. Children Playing with Skipping Rope. [Photograph] (2018). https://www.istockphoto.com/ca/photo/children-playing-with-skipping-rope-gm950604826-259470222
93	Rusli, Gaddafi. Playground. [Photograph] (2017). Image used under license from Unsplash. https://unsplash.com/photos/Y93IrZDfxmI

94	gargantiopa. Bird-eye view of the playground kids. [Photograph] (2019). https://www.istockphoto.com/ca/photo/bird-eye-view-of-the-playground-kids-gm1145559201-308374533
95	Geber86. Grandfather and granddaughter riding in a bus. [Photograph] (2016). Image used under license from iStock. https://www.istockphoto.com/ca/photo/grandfather-and-granddaughter-riding-in-a-bus-gm627101866-110990253
97	LSOphoto. Group of kids on the school background having fun. [Photograph] (2019). Image used under license from iStock. https://www.istockphoto.com/ca/photo/group-of-kids-on-the-school-background-having-fun-gm1176556884-328077633
98	bewakoofofficial. [Untitled Photograph] (2017). Image used under license from Unsplash. https://unsplash.com/photos/mG-HdjYiPtE/info
99	Sasiistock. Back to School. [Photograph] (2018). Image used under license from iStock. https://www.istockphoto.com/ca/photo/asian-pupil-kids-with-backpack-running-and-going-to-school-together-gm1011642586-272574181
100	Llamas, Jose. [Untitled Photograph] (2018). Image used under license from Unsplash. https://unsplash.com/photos/_8hHDCRwFJc/info
101	EvgeniiAnd. Child running on crosswalk. [Photograph] (2019). Image used under license from iStock. https://www.istockphoto.com/ca/photo/child-running-on-crosswalk-gm1130595734-299066975
102	Kristin Agnello, 2019
103	StockPlanets. Little boy riding bicycle on a running track. [Photograph] (2017). Image used under license from iStock. https://www.istockphoto.com/ca/photo/child-running-on-crosswalk-gm1130595734-299066975
107	Lilia Agnello, 2019
111	Du Preez, Priscilla. "Woman holding girl while learning to walk taken at daytime." (2017). Image used under license from Unsplash. https://unsplash.com/photos/3CTufp-cpzo
112	Blăjan, Alex. "Man and woman sitting on grass field during daytime." (2017). Image used under license from Unsplash. https://unsplash.com/photos/Vxv8sjOk_zY
114	Alphacolor. [Untitled Photograph] (2017). Image used under license from Unsplash. https://unsplash.com/photos/ipmwlGIXzcw
116	Benson, Chris. [Untitled Photograph] (2017). Image used under license from Unsplash. https://unsplash.com/photos/h0UG2Bd_Few
117	jeshoots. "Boy standing while reading map." (2017). Image used under license from Unsplash. https://unsplash.com/photos/LKREcvZeoJQ
119	neonbrand. "Man and woman sitting on chairs." (2017). Image used under license from Unsplash. https://unsplash.com/photos/zFSo6bnZJTw
122	Da Rosa, Jessica. "Woman sitting on chair." (2019). Image used under license from Unsplash. https://unsplash.com/photos/wXJViXxHP44
COVER	oska25. *Two girls sit at the bus stop stock photo.* [Photograph] (2017). Image used under license from iStock. https://www.istockphoto.com/ca/photo/two-girls-sit-at-the-bus-stop-gm653845774-118809449

CPSIA information can be obtained
at www.ICGtesting.com
Printed in the USA
BVRC090344280123
657299BV00005B/86